Au Pairing Up™

by

Ruth K. Liebermann

ISBN 0 - 918321 - 66 - 2

Publisher's Note:

This publication (in both print and electronic format) is designed to provide accurate and authoritative information in regard to the subject matter covered. It is sold with the understanding that the publisher is not engaged in rendering psychological or legal or other professional services. If expert assistance or psychological or legal counseling is needed, the services of a competent professional should be sought, in addition to the assistance of the organization that provided the au pair match.

Au Pairing Up™

P.O. Box 5405

Magnolia, MA 01930 - 0006

www.aupairingup.com

Printed in the United States of America

Dedication

This book is dedicated with love and affection to my family — our kids, Ethan and Nyssa, who have grown up to be terrific young adults and have been supportive in so many ways to my working in general, and to my husband, Tom, who is a whirlwind of action and inspires me to achieve much more than I ever think I am capable of accomplishing.

I am also thankful for the help from the 20 au pairs who have each shared about a year of their lives with our family.

— Ruth Liebermann

Table of Contents

Why I Wrote This Book

Hi! I'm Ruth Liebermann:

Wife, loving partner, mother, friend, girl scout leader, side line cheerleader, chauffeur, corporate HR "stiff," cleaning staff, first mate, cook, and chief bottle washer — you name it!

Like many mothers and most parents today, I wear lots of hats, and keep many of them balanced on my head simultaneously. Growing up in the '60's and '70's, I thought I could "have it all" — career, marriage, family, super womanhood. But somehow, just when I'd think everything was in carefully planned balance, one of my delicately placed chapeaus would fall out of line, and chaos would result.

One crazed early morning, my life went "tilt" one time too many, and I knew I needed help. The answer, of course, was composed of a number of changes, not a single magic pill. But relative to our children and childcare, the balancing equation has been hosting, for the past 16 years, a succession of live-in au pairs.

I won't lie to you and tell you they were all "Mary Poppins," because they were not. But I can share with you the wisdom of those years of experience and the perspective it's given me about how to handle the au pair experience with elan. It is the great injustice of life that we must live through a whole series of tough lessons to learn from them. However, you can benefit from my mistakes, and my successes, with 20 au pairs — and learn to avoid the former and duplicate the latter!

The kernel of this book is the "Standard Operating Procedure." This is the "Employee's Manual" that teaches your au pair about the management of your family, your children, your daily lives. Early on, I began to write this information down for each au pair, and review and edit it year to year as our lives, circumstances and needs changed. Writing the additional material that you need to complement this "Au Pair's Operating Manual" has been a natural extension of the years living the experience, enhanced by human resource management practices.

I hope this book will significantly demystify the au pair experience for many more families and for more potential au pairs. My expectation is to improve the slope and speed of the average user's learning curve in successfully selecting and hosting an au pair.

Why have an au pair? There are many reasons, but most importantly, our lives and our children's lives have been broadened through this exchange. The world is getting smaller every day, and we have been part of that in our growing understanding and tolerance of different cultures living together in a family setting. My hope is that you too will read through this book and decide to live this experience, but to do it in a more informed way than I did, when I first embarked on this most fascinating — and most helpful — international adventure.

Good luck and enjoy!

Benefits of "The Au Pair Solution™"

There are both pros and cons to having an au pair. Obviously, all things considered, my family believes that the live-in au pair arrangement is a worthwhile childcare alternative.

Many people's first reaction to our having a young adult from Europe living with us is, "How do you deal with having a stranger living in your home?" Our sense, after 16 years, is that the inherent breach in privacy is more than compensated for by the international social experience it provides our children and our family and the very real convenience of having someone there when needed.

As a teenager in the 1960s, my only regular source of pocket money was babysitting. Teenage schedules and commitments today do not leave much room for, or generate much interest in, babysitting. Plus, finding a list of totally reliable teenagers can be a challenge. One's ability to commit to social engagements, as well as to carry on a career, are seriously constrained by the challenge of finding dependable child care. And in addition the au pair can be available to help in unexpected occasions (as long as you don't overdo it).

The continuity of a single caregiver certainly adds to our comfort level on a day-to-day basis. Living as part of our family, the au pair knows what the pattern of each day demands. If there is a book report due, an illustrated poster to prepare, or a math quiz, the au pair knows the role she must play in our absence. With a few quick instructions and our destination and a contact phone number posted on the bulletin board, we can go on with commitments knowing that our children are with someone they live with and know.

Privacy is somewhat compromised but, managed with sensitivity to everyone's need for his or her own space, the advantages outweigh any inconveniences. Additionally, the children learn how to get along with different types of people.

The U.S. has long had the unique advantage of a common language in a large geographic territory. As globalization becomes a reality and information flows freely across the world, the need to co-exist with a variety of cultures at work, at play, and in family situations is the new reality. Our children have come to realize, better than we did as children, the unique gift of being multilingual and being "at home" with varying cultures. Living daily in a family situation with individuals whose language and life experiences are different from ours has provided my children, my husband, and me with invaluable learning opportunities.

How to Use This "Au Pairing Up™" Method

You don't need to read the entire book from start to finish at one sitting. Rather, a good strategy would be to start out by reading the first "general" sections in Part One.

When you are ready to put in an application, read Part Two, which will help you create an application which will bring you the best-suited au pair for your particular family.

After you've put in your application, read Part Three, which will help you to make the most informed selection from the applicants.

Now you'll be ready to read Part Four and prepare yourself, your family, and your soon-to-be au pair for the year in advance!

While you're awaiting your au pair's arrival, you'll have time to read Part Five and create a "Standard Operating Procedure" manual (your "SOP" — more on this in the next section). In Part Six, you'll also begin organizing the schedules, maps, task lists, and other elements of the "Au Pair Solution" that will make the experience as smooth and easy as it can be.

This will also be a good time to read Part Seven, with additional hints and suggestions for getting off on the right foot and working most cooperatively with your new au pair.

Part Eight will help you troubleshoot some common problems, and Part Nine will bring your au pair year to a successful close for both you and your au pair, and help you to prepare for your next one!

At the end of the book are hard copies of the charts and forms on the CD-ROM and other additional material that you will find useful.

About the CD-ROM

The CD-ROM contains charts and forms that I've created over the years and shared with other families using the Au Pair Solution. Feedback from these other host families has helped me to refine these tools. Perhaps most importantly, the CD-ROM contains customizable SOP "templates"which will allow you to customize them to fit your family's specific needs, simply by "filling in the blanks." Plus, you can print out as many charts, templates, or SOP's as you like. Complete instructions for doing so are included on the CD-ROM.

What Is a Standard Operating Procedure Manual (the SOP)?

A Standard Operating Procedure manual ("SOP") is simply human resource professional jargon for a set of standardized procedures that tells each employee of a company what is expected of him or her. The clearer and more detailed the SOP, the easier and faster it usually is for a new employee to come up to functioning speed.

The CD-ROM will help you create your own customized Standard Operating Procedure manual (SOP). Having a clearly written SOP already in place when your au pair arrives (an SOP that reflects *your* family's needs) is the biggest advantage you can have in beginning your au pair experience!

Other Charts and Forms: Paper and/or CD-ROM Versions

Other charts and forms include the following:

- An "Au Pair Spec Letter" to help you convey your specific needs to the agency

- A Post Arrival Checklist to help you organize those all-important early days

- A Weekly Schedule Activity Chart to show your au pair the repeated tasks of each day

- A Daily Activity Chart for Your Au Pair, with sections for each child and chore, specific to that day, with spaces for "unusual" or nonrepetitive tasks

- A "Four Weeks at a Glance" Chart, as well as a "Monthly" variation
- A "Year at a Glance" Chart, to show vacations, special days, etc.
- An easy format Emergency Phone Chart — which alone could be worth the price of the book!
- An "Au Pair Arrival Announcement" to help enlist the aid of teachers and parents of children's friends in helping the new au pair to feel welcome
- Shopping Charts, to tell your au pair where to buy what, with directions
- A General Phone List: relatives, family friends, merchants, service people
- A Children's Phone List: teachers, friends, lessons, etc.
- A Repeated Task Form: From music lessons to play dates, including what needs to be done, how to do it, where to go, what to bring, etc.
- An Easy Format Recipe Chart: what to make when, and where to find the recipe
- A Reference Letter, to help the departing au pair with subsequent career pursuits
- A Metric and Money Conversion Chart: includes distance and weight approximation

Most of these charts and forms are provided in two formats. They are on the CD-ROM for you to customize and print out, as well as at the end of the book for you to photo-copy and fill in.

Now it's time to go on to Part One of Au Pairing Up™!

PART ONE: Au Pairing Up™

Grammar and Gender

Au pairs are both male and female, although female au pairs are far more usual. However, if your children are male, you may certainly want an au pair of the same sex. For purposes of grammatical if not political correctness, we have chosen to use the pronoun "her" unless specifically referring to a male au pair.

What IS an Au Pair?

Au pair is French for "on a par," meaning "on a par with the rest of the family." Imagine subsidizing a distant young relative from a foreign country for a year, who will help you out, while learning about the U.S. An au pair can oversee and enrich your children's playtime and lives with the added dimension of another cultural perspective. This experience can provide the basis for a lifelong relationship.

An au pair is also:

- A J-1 Cultural Exchange Visa holder (nonemployee) for 12 months;
- a visiting member of your family; and
- an extra pair of hands available for up to 45 hours per week, (no more than 10 hours per day spread over up to 5 1/2 days per week) of childcare and light housekeeping.

An au pair's duties can include:

- preparing children's meals and cleaning up afterwards;
- making children's beds;
- straightening children's rooms;
- doing children's laundry;
- picking up children's belongings;
- driving children to school, lessons, appointments, outings, errands, etc.; and
- keeping her own room and doing her own laundry.

What an Au Pair is NOT!

An au pair is NOT:

- an employee.
- a stranger in your home, but is an extended member of your family.
- a replacement for caring and loving parent(s) . The au pair supplements the parents' ongoing presence and support.
- responsible on a regular basis for 24-hour care for children while you travel away from home overnight. These occasions must be very rare with plenty of backup support available.

- cheap, since you have to pay placement fees and a weekly stipend, as well as foot the bills for tickets, food, room, car/auto insurance, etc. (but consider the convenience and the cost of this flexible childcare alternative).

- a prisoner in your home. The au pair must be given ample time off and the means (e.g., use of car, means of transportation) to attend classes, meet with friends, attend cluster meetings with other au pairs, join your family for outings, etc.

- responsible for heavy housekeeping. She should not be responsible for general housekeeping, pet care, window washing, scrubbing floors, gardening, or other labor for the general household.

Now that you have a sense of what an au pair is, and is not, you need to think through your needs and the needs of your family relative to your suitability as applicants to this cultural exchange program. Your commitment to and responsibility for making this exchange a worthwhile experience for a visitor from another country are as important to the program as the personality and character of the au pair candidate with whom you are matched.

Comments from Families and Au Pairs

Throughout this book, we'll insert some comments from families with au pair experience, as well as a few from au pairs themselves. We'll format these so that you can tell at a glance whether they are from a child, an au pair, or a host parent. Here are a few that offer insight into why people are "Au Pairing Up!"

"Practically speaking it is an extra pair of hands, offers flexibility, consistency and continuity, reliability, good company, language development." — Host Parent

"Our au pair is fun to play with and helps me with my homework." — Host Kid

"I think I changed a lot with my year away as an Au Pair. I grew a lot stronger as a person. I no longer think it's that big of a deal to make contact with new people. And I have a lot more self confidence." — Au Pair

"We decided on this type of childcare because of the exposure it offers to other cultures." — Host Parent

"I am learning how to say things in another language." — Host Kid

"The best part of the experience for me was when I realized how much my English was improving. It felt great!" — Au Pair

"It offers an exciting opportunity for learning as a family and for the children as individuals." — Host Parent

"Our au pair from Sweden was happy and cheerful and fun to play with and taught us gymnastics." —Host Kid

"I think I'm in heaven!!! I've found a store with USA imports only! Jello, cheerios, Shake'N'Bake, real peanut butter, baking mixes (YES) you name it!" — Au Pair

The Au Pair Solution

If you are reading this book, you probably have already decided to get an au pair. But, like anything else in life, there are many different ways to get to the Au Pair Solution. The following sections will help you to make the au pair process a "win-win" situation for all parties after your au pair arrives.

Au Pair Issues

Three of the main general areas that can be problematic for the host of an au pair are control needs, privacy needs, and communication style. No matter what your position on these issues are, the Au Pair Solution may still work for you. However, you may have to make sure that certain needs (such as privacy) are considered in advance, or that certain issues (such as your communication style) are modified.

Control and privacy issues can best be addressed by creating a customized Standard Operating Procedure manual (SOP) with the help of the CD-ROM. Hints and tips on communication are described in the following section. Learning to "read between the lines" of an au pair application may also help you choose the candidate who will fit best with your family.

Communication Issues

Everyone has a unique style of communication. Some of us are very direct and quick to discuss problems or issues with the other people involved. Some of us prefer to avoid bringing up problems for discussion. Some are quick to praise, others quicker to blame or find fault. And for many parents, communication about a child may be different (and probably more emotional and protective) from their "normal" communication style.

It is crucial to communicate clearly and in a straightforward fashion with your au pair, especially since English may not be her first language. More communication suggestions will be provided in the sections entitled "Communication in General" (page 112) and "Weekly Review" (page 109).

Privacy Issues

Obviously, you will need to have sufficient space to house your au pair, with at least one small private room. Less obviously, your own (or your spouse's and children's) needs for personal space and privacy also must be taken into account. Getting used to having an additional adult, with her own needs and habits, will require some give and take on both sides. Some of these issues can be finessed with a modicum of advance thought.

If you or your spouse have specific privacy needs, you may want to customize your SOP on the CD-ROM to address this issue. For example, if one TV in the house is connected to cable (and thus all the sports stations), you may decide that when the host father is home, his preference for channel, remote control, and his favorite chair come first. You may also decide to deal with an issue of this nature by having an extra TV in the au pair's room. Additional suggestions regarding privacy issues can be found in the SOP.

Control Issues

Some people have a strong need to be in control, others less so. By observing yourself at work or interacting with your family, you'll be able (if you've never considered it before) to see where you fit on the "high/low control scale."

If you have a high need for control, you will want to be very specific in the SOP about how you want things done so that your instructions can be followed easily to your satisfaction. You will also want to be clear about the attributes you need in your au pair when you write your "spec letter" to the agency (page 30).

Remember that your au pair comes to you as a young adult with a reasonably formulated personality. You will be able to change or control certain aspects of her behavior, but not all of them. So you'll need to "pick your battles" carefully. For instance, ragged blue jeans may not be an issue for you, but no cigarettes may be nonnegotiable.

If you are more laissez-faire in your attitude, don't be surprised if things get a bit lax in the household (unless, of course, you've clarified your desires in the ubiquitous SOP).

If You're a Couple

If you are in a spousal relationship, you will find it useful to discuss the previous section together. Doing so will identify issues for one partner that might not be obvious to the other (as shown in the "knockout" comment described below). It may also be useful in helping you decide who will be the main au pair contact (or whether both will). This exercise is not necessary for single parents, but could be important if another nonspousal adult is regularly in the home.

As you review each of the "au pair issues," ask yourselves the question: How might any difference in our feelings about these issues affect our family's relationship with an au pair?

"It may sound trite, but I have not wanted a very attractive au pair. As a third adult in the house, it is important to me that she not be a 'knockout'." — Host Parent

Your Family Style

How do you know what your family style is? Consider the following description:

• In authoritarian families, discipline is likely to be strict, and adherence to family rules of high importance. One person (usually with the highest control need in the family) is the decision maker, and the decisions flow from the top down. In some authoritarian families, both spouses form one "decision-making unit."

• A consensus family takes input from most or all members before making decisions.

• A laissez-faire style family tends to be very loose. Members are likely to "do their own thing" without too much discipline.

Most families are a combination of the style described. Thinking about your own family styles before you get an au pair will help you make the best selection.

In general, families who do best with this type of childcare arrangement are those who are interested in sharing and giving in this experience as well as broadening themselves and their children's lives in the process. Personally, we welcome the au pair as a typical "big sister" into our family. We encourage the au pair to join our family activities, or to do "her own thing" during her spare time. We likewise ask our children to treat the au pair like their "big sister" and the au pair to treat our children as she would her own sister or brother. As one host child puts it:

"I like having a friend around all the time. She also introduces me to other cultures that I don't know anything about." — Host Kid

The Golden Rules of Thumb

No matter who you are or what style family you have there are a few Golden Rules that every successful au pair family that I've known follows. They are so important that I will introduce them now and refer to them often.

Golden Rule #1: Everyone — adults, kids, and the au pair — should work as hard as possible to make it work.

Golden Rule #2: Deal with things as they arise.

Now it's time to go on to Part Two, and learn about The Application Process.

PART TWO: The Application Process

The National Au Pair Organizations

Over the dozen-plus years we have had au pairs, we have worked with three different national organizations. There are currently only six national organizations designated by the U.S. Information Agency (USIA) to administer the Au Pair Program. The USIA has established and documented regulations for these programs and monitors their general adherence. Because all must comply with these regulations, the basic programs and fees among the six are relatively similar.

The six accredited programs and their contact addresses and phone, fax, and website/e-mail contact numbers are:

American Institute for Foreign Study
(Au Pair in America)

102 Greenwich Avenue	Tel.: (203) 869-9090	(800) 727-2437
Greenwich, CT 06830	Fax: (203) 863-6180	www.aifs.com

Au Pair Programme USA
(Childcrest)

6965 Union Park Center, Suite 100	Tel.: (801) 255-7722	Fax: (801) 255-7782
Medvale, UT 84047	www.childcrest.com	info@childcrest.com

YUSA International
(Au Pair Care)

455 Market St. 17th Fl.	Tel.: (415) 434-8788	(800) 428-7247
San Francisco, CA 94105	Fax: (415) 616-0585	

Educational Foundation for Foreign Study
(EF Au Pair)

One Education Street	Tel.: (617) 619-1100	(800) 333-6056
Cambridge, MA 02141	Fax: (617) 619-1101	aupair@ef.com

EurAuPair Intercultural
       Child Care Programs
105 Central Way, Suite 201   Tel.: (425) 803-3859/(800) 713-2002   Fax:(425) 828-1987
Kirkland, WA 98633   www.euraupair.com

InterExchange, Inc.
(Au Pair USA)
161 Sixth Avenue, 13th Fl.   Tel.: (212) 924-0446/(800) 287-2477   Fax:(212) 924-0575
New York, NY 10013   www.interexchange.org   interex@earthlink.net

Unaccredited Organizations and Unauthorized Au Pairs

You may remember news reports in early 1993 of Clinton's first presidential admin-
istration of a proposed appointment to Attorney General of Zoe Baird, a female lawyer,
general counsel for Aetna Life & Casualty of Hartford, Connecticut. Within days of the
initial news, this aspiring lawyer withdrew her name from consideration due to issues
raised about undocumented childcare workers in her family.

Although you may have no intention of running for Attorney General or any other
very visible public office, you should still find comfort, given the nuances of immigration
regulations, that departure visas and a smooth entry into and departure from the U.S. are
all prearranged through the national organizations and their affiliates. Hosting a foreign
visitor for a year through one of these federally sanctioned programs will give you, as the
hosting family, virtually no immigration difficulties. This is a good reason for choosing
one of the nationally recognized organizations.

Smaller Organizations and U.S. Born Au Pairs

Other smaller organizations exist in large metropolitan areas. Most of them source
local candidates or have connections to rural U.S. locales. Having spoken with a few of
them over the years, we have continued to seek the international flavor that an au pair
from outside the U.S. brings to our family. Although the personal attention these smaller
organizations offer has appeal, we have found the established program parameters of the
accredited agencies working with international au pairs to be much more reassuring. There
is also real retention value to the fact that a non-U.S. au pair's visa is directly related to her
continuing in this specific program. An American might feel more freedom to consider
other employment that her "bond" may not dissuade her from taking.

Size and Structure of the Organizations

Size varies some among these organizations and there has been some consolidation
of agencies within the past few years. With between 100 and 4,000 families and their related au pairs to serve, the personal touch that each agency offers can certainly vary, and it
can make a difference.

Where the Au Pairs Come From

The au pair programs draw most of their candidates from outside the U.S., typically through a network of alliances with student exchange organizations in various countries. These organizations advertise the au pair programs in local magazines. Upon inquiry, a personal interview is arranged and the process of identifying potential au pair candidates begins.

The cultural phenomenon of au pairs had been centered in Europe until the mid-1980s when student exchange programs in the U.S. started expanding into au pair programs as another "exchange" product. In that time, more than 70,000 families in the U.S. have had au pairs. It is estimated that each year about 12,000 au pairs come the the U.S. through the six national organizations.

A number of au pairs who have lived with us indicated that their mothers had had au pair experiences within Europe as young adults. Often it offered a means of strengthening another foreign language capability as well as experiencing another European culture without traveling too far from home (a young German woman as an au pair to a French family for the summer, for example).

Because, European education paths are defined earlier in one's "gymnasium"/high school years than they are in the U.S., young Europeans are more likely to take time off between high school and a job or pursuing university studies to travel or seek out a cultural exchange experience of some sort. Coming to the U.S., and experiencing firsthand its language and culture within the comfort of a family for one year with little out-of-pocket cost (a $500 refundable "bond") is an attractive, relatively risk-free way to learn about the country and expand one's horizons.

"It's just awesome to remember all the stuff I had the opportunity to do with all you "guys". I just had the time of my life. I have to admit that I really miss the enthusiasm and positive atmosphere at the Liebermann family. Somehow, everything seemed easier with you, and many more things seemed possible....." — Au Pair

"Au Pair Speak": Some Definitions

Following are a few labels for people and subgroups within the programs. Knowing these definitions in advance may be convenient.

• **Cluster** — defines a geographic area within which a local coordinator is responsible for a group of host families and their respective au pairs. The cluster, within any single organization, becomes the most immediate, known "circle" for your au pair to become acquainted with other young adults also participating in this exchange program.

• **Local Coordinator** — a designated adult who has formal responsibility within a cluster of local program coordination, for an organization. This can include interviewing prospective families, coordinating meetings/get-togethers of the cluster's au pairs, answering questions about the program, and general trouble-shooting.

• **Regional Coordinator** — regionally based adult who may oversee a few local coordinators, assisting them in their interface with the organization and the overall program and its development.

What to Look For

The national organizations differ only slightly in their actual programs. The differences you experience more, as a family, are closer to home in terms of

- what penetration/concentration your agency has in your surrounding communities with other au pair placements/host families
- who your local coordinators are; and
- how active the local coordinators are in getting the au pairs together to have some shared experiences during their year in the U.S.

"We selected the organization we are working with by the good following and reputation of our local coordinator. She is a dynamo and I was impressed with her manner and honesty on the phone the first time we spoke." — Host Parent

Local Support

Through adult education classes or the local "Y" sports club, your au pair will likely meet other au pairs in reasonable proximity to you. It does not matter if they are from different organizations. What matters is that your au pair meet other young people in similar circumstances with whom she can share new experiences.

If your local coordinator arranges some fun events during the course of the year that is a bonus. It is most important that your au pair be in contact with and identify with other young people, either to speak her own language or simply share new impressions. These peer relationships are critical for nurturing your au pair during her stay and for ensuring "local" carryover value as each family transitions to new au pairs. The more au pairs there are in your geographic area, the larger the circle of friends your au pair will have to draw on, and the happier she will likely be overall.

"At Christmas, I got a really nice card from Ruth Rudrecos, do you remember? She was the Au Pair of the Stimpels at the same time when I was with you. We didn't hear from each other since about 4 or 5 years or so. So we will get in contact again. Probably we can meet this year sometime in London or Paris...."
— Au Pair

Your Family's Au Pair "Spec"

In a business, when defining the exact characteristics of a product you are having made to order, you give the manufacturer a "spec" (short for "specification") sheet. The spec sheet tells the manufacturer the precise function, size, color, shape, and other qualities and characteristics of the product that you want delivered.

It is critical that you think through what the ideal "spec" is for you and your family relative to an au pair. Your considerations should range from the most basic (such as whether you want a male or female au pair and what an ideal age would be) to the more subtle, such as a sense of what you would be looking for in an au pair's family background. You may want to consider questions such as the following:

- Is the candidate currently living with both parents?

- What type of work do the parents do?

- Does the candidate have other siblings — sisters? brothers? what age ? where is the candidate in the sibling order?

- What responsibilities does the candidate currently have in her own home?

- What type of previous childcare experience does the candidate have? What age children has the candidate previously cared for?

Considering Your Family's Needs

PLUS

the Candidates Background

EQUALS

A "Best Fit" Match

Clarify Your Needs, Then Define Your Family's "Au Pair Spec"

You must be clear about what works for your family, and the type of person that best suits your needs (see an example spec on page 30). Then, be as direct and clear as possible about your desires with your local coordinator, the au pair candidates, and finally the national agency.

Develop a firm sense of what will work for you and what will not and what the personality characteristics are that would most lend themselves to success in your family. The more trust you have in your local coordinator and her/his understanding of you and your family, the better your matches will be overall. Presenting the agency with a clear and honest application will help immensely (see page 32).

A successful match cannot be guaranteed, but you can take comfort in knowing that the coordinator oversees 15 to 20 of these matches per year and has often developed a "sixth sense" of the chemistry your circumstance requires.

The following section will make it easy for you to think about, then decide on, your own au pair spec. Use the template on the CD-ROM to print it out and send it to the agency.Enlisting children to help with this (or at least some of the questions, such as "special interests") will help to give them a sense of ownership in the process, if they are old enough to understand the issues involved.

Host Family—Developing Your Au Pair Spec

As you are completing the au pair spec of your host family application, consider and discuss as a couple or as a family the items listed below to clarify what type of individual you seek and the values and interests you want to concentrate on in your selection. The material in parentheses will help you to understand the issues underlying each element of your spec.

This spec work will be very germane to reading candidate applications, considering matches, and deciding which individuals would best suit your family. Develop your own definitive (either/or) questions. Otherwise, an eager au pair who really wants the job may answer yes to everything.

Gender

Au pair must be   Female_____   Male_____   Either_____

(You may want to complement your unique "single mother with boys" circumstance with a male au pair to provide the balance of another male in your family dynamic. Or, you may have two active male children for whom you feel another male would be the best match.)

Age of Ideal Candidate

18 to 21____   21 to 23____   23 to 25____

(Think about the qualities of youthfulness versus maturity relative to your children's needs. With toddlers, you may want a more youthful au pair who will crawl on the floor, playing "peek-a-boo." Consider what the varied objectives might be for an older au pair, who is taking a year away on an exchange in her early 20s. What had she been doing in her home country and what might she be expecting to get out of the year away?)

"Our children are still quite small. I need a playful, youthful au pair who will get down on the floor and play with them, at their level." — Host Parent

Candidate's Family

(What the candidate has been used to is likely what she is best at.)

Other siblings: # of brothers___   ages ____   # of sisters___ ages___

(You may not want a candidate who is the oldest of four sisters taking care of your four boys. Once again, consider, "what is this person used to?")

The applicant currently lives with both parents__ with mother__ with father__ with friends___ alone___ other _____(please specify)

(The candidate's current living arrangement can give you a sense of her family dynamic. If the candidate is not living with her parents, it may indicate a certain level of independence and adaptability in terms of living in a new family situation.)

Do both parents work outside the home ? _____
Parents jobs: Blue collar_____   White collar_____ professional_____

(Candidates' socioeconomic situations can be indicative of their upbringing and expectations. Again, keep in mind, that what they themselves have experienced is what they are used to, and what they will be best at. Candidates with at-home mothers who have been doing everything for them, may be less familiar with many of the needs you may have for them in your family. Then again, a child of a middle class family may be more facile in social interaction and have more polished manners, which may fit your lifestyle better.)

What type of relations does the candidate have with other extended family members? Aunts and uncles? Cousins? Grandparents?

(These relationships will give you some sense of the importance of "family" in the candidate's upbringing.)

What type of responsibilities has the candidate had at home?

(Again, what the candidate is used to is what she will be best at. If she was never responsible for getting a dinner together at home, you will likely need to make a number of meals together before she is comfortable "on her own" in the kitchen getting a healthy, balanced meal out regularly for your children.)

"We are a two-career family with four children. There is a fair amount of sibling interaction and rivalry and a very active household. It is important to me that our au pair come from a family with a few siblings, preferably sisters and brothers (we have both), as well as having both parents working outside the home. With this basic dynamic, there is more likelihood that the au pair candidate has had basic household responsibilities and has an understanding of what is required to keep a household running effectively with everyone 'pitching in.'"

— Host Parent

Region of Origin Preference

(These observations are my own and while possibly overly generalized, are somewhat valid at least.)

England, Scotland, Ireland, Australia, New Zealand_____

(English is clearly their first language. In fact, like many Americans, they may not be fluent in any other language. They may lack a certain warmth, and tend to believe the adage "children should be seen and not heard.")

Northern Europe_____ (Sweden, Denmark, Norway, Germany (West or East), Austria, Belgium, Switzerland, Holland)

(Other than language, more like Americans.)

Southern Europe_____ (southern France, Spain, Italy)

(At the risk of being overly generalizing, candidates from this area tend to be more easy-going. Italians and Spanish tend to be more expressive, more demonstrative, warmer toward children.)

Central Europe____ (Hungary, Romania, Poland, the Czech Republic, Slovakia, Slovenia, Latvia, Russia, Finland)

(Regular driving experience may be an issue. They are likely to be very impressed by the relative opulence of the U.S. They tend to be very mindful of authority and open to doing whatever is asked of them.)

Central America____   South America____Mexico_____

(Not , as yet, an abundant candidate channel.)

North America: Northeast____   Southeast___ Southwest___ Midwest___Northwest___ Canada____

(Not a source for the six national organizations.)

"Because, as host mother, I speak another European language that we want to share with our children, a critical characteristic for our family is that the first language of the au pair we host be my native tongue and that the individual is willing to support our desire to strengthen this foreign language skill with our children." — Host Parent

Religion

Most applications will ask you your religion and how religious you and your family are.

(Consider your own religious proclivities and whether it is important that an au pair be of the same or a similar religion. Will you expect an au pair to attend services with you? If so, would you expect her to be a participant or only an observer? If your family is not religious, will it be a problem if the au pair is?

Some families find having an au pair with a different religion part of the broadening experience. Others find that having an au pair of the same religion (but from a different country) enhances their family's understanding of their own religion.)

Ages of Your Children

(A candidate's age group preference is most critical in terms of what the au pair's responsibilities will be)

Would want candidate to prefer this age group of children to care for:

Newborn _____

(For children below the age of 1, especially if both parents are working full time outside the home, it is not recommended that an au pair be considered the sole source of childcare. We recommend that the au pair's services be complemented with at least one other additional childcare alternative for some number of hours each week.)

1 to 2_____   3 to 5 _____   6 to 10 _____   11 to 15_____

(For the older age group, you are striving for a "big sister" relationship. Look for a candidate whose experience lends itself to her being a buddy, yet also a guiding mature young adult.)

"As our children are now middle school age, it's become more important that our au pair be older, at least 21 years of age, so our children recognize this person as an adult." — Host Parent

Driving Experience

How long has the candidate had a driver's license? Years ___ Months___

Most of the candidate's driving experience has been   Rural___ City___ Suburban___ Highway___

How often does the candidate drive per week ?

(Will driving responsibility be a small or big part of the regular household routine? What amount of driving will be required and where? A young adult driving a family vehicle can raise important issues regarding safety and the costs involved. The au pair should understand the significant value of driving and its related responsibilities.)

"Our home is in a lovely, but somewhat remote suburb. Daily driving is crucial. Because of this, I look for candidates with a few years of frequent driving experience." — Host Parent

Interests

Candidate has highest preference for   Music___ Art___ Sports___ Other___

Candidate's interests/activities in spare time Active ____ (sports, dance clubs) More Passive____ (reading, movies, crafts)

(Consider the interests of your family. How do you spend your spare time? How do you typically entertain — formal/ informal, planned/ spontaneous?)

"We have a swimming pool in our yard and the children spend much of the summer in the pool. It is vital that our au pairs be very capable swimmers." — Host Parent

Some Thoughts on Personality

Think for a few moments about the personality of the au pair who will best fit into your family. When you read the applications and do the phone interviews, you can attempt to pick a personality type that will be appropriate, or (perhaps just as important) eliminate a candidate whose personality will not mesh well with your family. If you live with a spouse or other adults, you may wish them to fill it out as well, and compare your answers. As you can see, circling a "1" on the "Flexible to Determined" scale would indicate that you prefer someone who is very flexible, and circling a "7" would indicate a preference for someone very determined. A "3" would be in the middle of the "Flexible to Determined" scale, but a bit more on the flexible side.

Do you want someone who is:

Flexible	1	2	3	4	5	6	7	Determined
Patient	1	2	3	4	5	6	7	Deliberate
Quiet	1	2	3	4	5	6	7	Outgoing
Reflective	1	2	3	4	5	6	7	Inquisitive
Trusting	1	2	3	4	5	6	7	Confrontive
Serious	1	2	3	4	5	6	7	Playful
Polite	1	2	3	4	5	6	7	Outspoken

Spec Letter to Agency (Liebermann)

The spec letter helps you convey your specific needs to the agency. If you are concerned about specific issues, this is a good format for highlighting your needs, as the following letter does. This family needs an au pair who will make a good impression during the business vacations that the family takes, thus the emphasis on presentability and manners.

ATTN: Program Director

Subject: Reactivation forms/fees, etc.

Dear Program Director:

Our family has had another GREAT au pair year.

It has been our experience that there are quite specific characteristics that are very important in a successful au pair match for us, a family with two school-age children and with both parents very active in business and social functions, some involving travel as a family.

The qualities that seem to be good indicators of success for us are these:

- Female
- Northern European
- Family background: mother and father living together, more than one child in family, middle class family, preferably well traveled
- "Family" is important to au pair
- Makes a good personal presentation, has good manners and social skills
- Is used to interacting with adults in social situations
- Is active (Sports, hobbies, studies, etc.)
- Is self-assured, responsible, honest, mature, shows some independence
- Is 21 years of age or older
- Is an experienced automobile driver
- Is a good swimmer
- Doesn't smoke

We are sorry to see this year end, but are hopeful [Agency] can repeat this success.

Thank you.

Sincerely,
Ruth Liebermann

Att./rkl
cc: Local coordinator

Spec Letter to Agency (Generic)

Here is a generic copy of a spec letter to an agency, which you can fill out in long-hand if you like. However, the version on the CD-ROM will make it easier to take the results of your "Au Pair Spec Research" and convert it to letter form.

ATTN: (Program Director)
(Au Pair Agency)

Subject: Qualities Desired in Our Au Pair

Dear (Program Director):

Following is a description of the qualities that we think will be important to us in choosing an au pair.

- Sex:
- Country of Origin:
- Age Range:
- Family Background:
- Personal Presentation:
- General Activity Level:
- Athletic Abilities:
- Additional Personal Qualities
- Driving Experience:
- Religious Preferences:
- Smoker/Non-Smoker
- Other Issues:

We look forward to seeing the matches that you suggest.

Sincerely,

Your Host Family Application

Once you've decided on an agency and developed your own spec, you will need to fill out a written application. Most organizations include a blank application form with their printed materials.

Read through the application first before filling it in to be clear what is required and what you can draw from in the work and thinking you have already done. There will undoubtedly be sections probing your family interests, the community in which you live, your typical weekly schedule, whether you spend weekends and vacations somewhere specific, etc. Draw from the work you have already done through this workbook and represent your family and your needs directly and honestly.

The materials requested by each organization are slightly different but may include:

- Basic written three to four page application (will require a signature agreeing to the terms of the program)
- Family essay describing yourselves, your children, the general household schedule, goals for the children , expectations in hosting an au pair, your sense of what the most important ingredients are for success within this program (will often require some photographs of your family)
- Specific information about your community, access to educational institutions, the arts, a metropolitan city, public transportation
- Confidential friend, neighbor, possibly your employer, recommendation letters
- Deposit (submitting the application will likely require an administrative fee to secure your commitment)

The Liebermann Family Essay

Here is an example of a sample family essay that is quite comprehensive in describing all the members of the household; the basic schedule of the family and its activities; and the basic "look and feel" of the home, the neighborhood, and its surroundings. While you read this, think of how you would represent your family to a potential au pair candidate. Most application forms will also ask you to include specific information on any physical or mental handicaps involving family members in residence.

Family Essay

Let me describe to you a little about each of the four of us:

I was raised in central Connecticut (a neighboring state to Massachusetts, also in new England) as the second of three children in a second-generation Polish-American family. I had an active childhood with lots of exposure to sports, the arts, music, etc. After college, I lived in New York City for three-and-a-half years, eventually completing my graduate studies there at Columbia University.

After finishing my master's degree in business, I moved to southern Indiana for a professional position with a large industrial corporation. I met Tom there, and after dating and wondering for three years whether we would have ever noticed each other in New York City or Philadelphia, we were married. Three years later we had our son, and after another three years, our daughter. Having married in our late 20s, we had the opportunity to devote time to successful careers and fully enjoy our 20s as independent adults. My husband, our children, and family in general are very important to me as is the stimulation of a professional work setting. With quality childcare and the assistance in running a busy household that an au pair provides, balancing both has been possible and extremely rewarding. My current professional responsibility is as a human resource director responsible for directing and coordinating compensation, benefits, and systems.

My husband came to the U.S. on his own at the age of 15, having emigrated with his family first from Romania to Israel, then on his own from Israel to Brookline, Massachusetts. He finished high school there and went to engineering and graduate business school at the University of Pennsylvania in Philadelphia, Pennsylvania, where he also played college and then professional soccer. He is a patriotic foreign-born American, hard driving and appreciative of all that he has experienced and achieved. A flavor of his Eastern European past exists in his slight accent and his drive for excellence. He has a terrific sense of humor, is extremely insightful about people, and is, not surprisingly, an excellent manager, husband and father. He is currently the chairman and chief executive officer of ASI, which invests in and manages industrial and medium-technology companies. My husband has an incredible supply of energy for the demands of his work and business-related commitments as well as for sports and family activities.

Our son, age 17, is a handsome, tall, great young man and a pretty typical first-born male child. He is sensitive, somewhat cautious in trying new things, hardworking at school and sports, and has a good sense of humor. His favorite sports that he participates in are tennis, basketball, skiing, lacrosse, soccer, swimming, and sailing. He has always enjoyed the company of other kids and is not one to keep himself occupied at length on his own. He is entering the 12th grade at the school he and his sister attend. This will be his final year at this school and he has an important year ahead of him academically, in sports, and in his thinking and decision making about what school he will attend for college.

Our daughter, age 13, is a cute "fireball." She is a fairly typical second child — is very self-confident and bright; plays well on her own; has many interests; enjoys music, playing games, playing cards and board games, art, reading, and baking. The activities she is involved with outside of school are gymnastics, tennis, Girl Scouts, swimming, sailing, basketball, soccer, and lacrosse. Our daughter takes piano lessons and enjoys singing.

Our goals for our son and daughter are: to provide a home environment that offers lots of love and caring. Through opportunities at home, at school, and outside of school, we hope to see them develop themselves to their fullest potential, with a strong sense of self confidence and trust in those around them and the world in general. We are encouraging the children to be as independent as is sensible, given their ages.

A typical weekday in our house would be like this:

6:00 a.m. : My husband and I get up

6:50: Au pair should be up and dressed and should awaken the children for school. Children shower, get dressed, get school bags gathered, and eat breakfast. Au pair should remind them to make their beds, brush teeth, and comb hair. My husband leaves for work or sports workout on the way to work.

7:00-7:15: I leave for work.

7:40: Au pair takes both children to school.

Typically, between this time and 10:30 a.m. the light housework responsibilities that the au pair has for that day would be taken care of . They might include a number of different things, including picking up children's rooms, clearing breakfast dishes, doing some food shopping, washing some clothing, doing light dusting or vacuuming, emptying dishwasher, watering houseplants, starting to prepare something for that evening's dinner, etc.

The au pair can expect to have free time between 10:30 a.m. and 2:00/3:30 p.m. or even longer if really efficient.

Furthermore, given frequent visits of grandparents and during family trips, the au pair has large blocks of time for herself. The au pair is encouraged to take full advantage of this picturesque part of America (including education and self-development) during these periods of time, especially given the availability of a third family car.

2:00 (Friday) / 3:30 p.m. (Monday—Thursday): Au pair picks up the children. Each day of the week is somewhat different ranging from going right home with the children, getting them a healthy snack and then having them sit down to their homework (while the au pair oversees this and finishes getting dinner ready), to some days when there are after school activities— (swimming, tennis, gymnastics, piano) when the au pair is getting the children where they need to be and back home again.

Only rarely during the week (because the children get quite a bit of homework), will the children have friends over or go to a friend's house. When that happens the au pair may drive them there or back.

7:00 p.m.: I return home.

7:00 -7:30: Eat dinner (with or without my husband, depending on his schedule).

7:15 -8:00: My husband returns home.

9:00-10:00: Kids start getting ready for bed. I often read at least to my daughter a story and "tuck children into bed."

10:30-12:00: My husband I go to bed.

We are an active, cheerful, and energetic family. There is always much to talk about, and the children are always looking for an audience for their stories and experiences, someone with whom they can actively share their lives and who will share theirs. We are casual entertainers— often making last-minute plans to have another family/couple/ visiting family join us for sailing, skiing, tennis, walking, biking, or for a quick meal that we have pulled together at the last minute, etc.

We are often "on the go" as a family and there is lots of spontaneity and energy in the household. You will have opportunities to travel to a few states with us and have some cultural experiences — theater, concerts, movies, etc. — with us and on your own. If interested, you can volunteer to help at some of the children's school programs and our daughter's girl scouts.

We had the good fortune to live in Holland for a year and a half, from 1983 to 1985. Through my husband's family and background, my ancestry, and a number of international friends and business associates, we regularly experience a multinational flavor in our lives. You, likewise, will be exposed in our home to many different kinds of people, often international.

Our home is a four-bedroom, three full bathrooms, split-entry garrison that sits on a small hill overlooking the Atlantic Ocean (400 yards away). Our backyard backs onto a cul-de-sac with seven other suburban homes.

[Our Town] was, after World War II, a small exclusive summer resort community with several lovely old hotels overlooking the ocean. A few of these historic buildings remain. The downtown street of [Our Town] (within half a mile of our house) has with the basics — post office, library, a few clothing stores, a small grocery store, restaurants, and a hairdresser. [Our Town] is part of [a Neighboring Town], with an overall population of 32,000 . [Our Town] itself has less than 5,000 people.

[Another Neighboring Town], a town of 5,500 people, is within one mile of our home. This is a quaint (regional area of U.S) community with a lovely harbor and small downtown area. Most of our activities center in [another Neighboring Town] — quick shopping, sailing, commuter railway service to [Major Metropolitan City]. Many people living in this area commute to [Major Metropolitan City] each day to work.

In summary, for more than 16 years, we have had au pairs living with us. We are a family interested in sharing and "giving" in this experience as well as broadening ourselves and our children's lives in the process. We feel strongly that the multidimensional flavor that a European au pair brings to our family is unmatched. The opportunity for a bilingual experience and the representation of a different background enriches all of our lives unlike any alternative.

We welcome the au pair as a typical "big sister" into our family. We encourage the au pair to join into our family activities or to do "her own thing" during her spare time. We ask the kids to treat the au pair like their "big sister," and we ask the au pair to treat them as she would her own sister or brother. We feel strongly that as a couple and family we offer a unique and rewarding experience to a visitor to this country.

WELCOME !

Host Family Confidential Reference

Most applications will require that you get a friend or neighbor to write a confidential reference. This will include their perspective on family relationships, the atmosphere for a potential au pair, any physical or mental handicaps or disorders of family members, and the existence, if any, of other serious problems (including drug or alcohol abuse, domestic violence, or sexual abuse).

Visit from the Local Coordinator

Once you have formally applied, you may next have a visit from the local coordinator in your region. The purpose of this visit is to meet and interview you in person, clarify any questions that may have come up through your family application and see your home and the accommodations you have for a visiting au pair. The local coordinator can be helpful in screening potential candidates for you from the agency and is certainly a worthwhile sounding board and "second opinion" on the profiles you will be reviewing. Get to know your local coordinator and use them to optimize your selection.

"Our current coordinator was herself an au pair a number of years ago. Being now a parent of young children herself, she has a strong sense of what the important characteristics are for a host family and for a potential au pair. She has been a tremendous help to us during the interviewing/matching process, having come to know our family and the au pairs we have hosted quite well over the years. She has a good 'sixth sense' of what type of individual best fits our family lifestyle and needs." — Host Parent

The coordinator may also ask for your input on available educational alternatives for an au pair to pursue. Program costs included a $500 educational stipend which the au pair must use to satisfy program requirements. Be thinking about what types of programs exist in your general area.

PART THREE: Choosing an Applicant

Reading Your Au Pair Applications

Once your application and in-home interview are complete, you will be hearing from the organization. You will either receive a match they feel best suits your needs or receive one or more applications from au pair candidates which you must review in order to decide if you wish to interview them further by phone.

It is crucial that you understand how your organization does the matching. Does the organization consider "matching" to be a key responsibility of theirs, or do they provide you, the host family, with applications they think may be a good matches but leave phone interviewing and the final selection up to you?

"Our organization prides itself in doing the 1-to-1 matching process internally and presenting the match to the host family. We feel we are in a good position to access the host family's needs, as specified in their application, with the pool of applicants we have available from which to select. The host family has the final say in the selection and we will talk it through with them and reconsider the match if the family does not agree with our choice."

— Au Pair Agency

Pay particular attention to the reports of the organization's initial interview of the candidate. Notice how they rate the candidate's English language capability. From the childcare references provided by the candidate, watch for the items rated somewhat lower and consider how the varied characteristics were ranked. Often these references are from a relative and may not be as objective as you might wish.

The applications are revealing on an elementary level even before you speak with the candidates by phone. You can generally get a sense of their ability to express themselves comfortably in English, a sense of cultural norms in terms of how they answer "what if" type questions, and their playfulness/creativity in how expressive they are in their personal letter and choice of photographs to share.

The written references provided by the candidates are only somewhat useful as is the agency's home country interview notes about the candidate and her English language proficiency. Understand the limitations of these pieces and do your best to round out your understanding of the candidate through your insightful phone interviewing (see page 40).

Other Perspectives: Get a Second Opinion

Read the application(s) from the candidate(s) you are considering a few times. Have your spouse or another adult who knows your family read the application(s) over also and get their opinion to balance and even counter your own. Often another person will notice things in the application that you did not. These varied perspectives are important. You want to "read between the lines" as much as you possibly can in this, your first glimpse at the candidate(s).

"We had an application from a young woman who indicated her willingness to care for disabled children. At first reading, that seemed a very giving perspective for a 20-year-old. Re-reading the application again and speaking by phone with this candidate, it became obvious that she was currently helping take care of her boyfriend's disabled brother and that this had clearly "earned her points" with the boyfriend. A bit of an ulterior motive and not the purely generous and understanding soul I had thought on first reading." — Host Parent

Tough Questions

Over the years, I have come to most appreciate those written applications that ask the "tough questions" — questions that describe situations that are likely to come up. From the candidates responses to such questions you can learn much about her, both personally and culturally. Following are some examples I have seen posed to the candidate:

- "You have made plans for the evening. The host mother calls and has been de layed by a meeting that will now extend through dinner and into the evening. You will have to stay home with the children tonight. How do you feel?"

- "The child gets ill. The host mother has said always to call her at the office before doing anything. You call and she is out of the office. What do you do in this situation?"

- "The baby you are caring for is asleep. You, however, urgently need something from the store in order to have the children's dinner ready on time, when the host mother comes home. What do you do?"

- "Your host family is very lax on discipline. They are against corporal punishment. One child behaves badly and deserves a spanking. What do you do?"

- "Your host family requires you to be home by 11 p.m. on weeknights when you will be working the following day. What is your reaction?"

You may want to ask these or similar queries in your phone interviews with the candidates.

It's Your Choice

Make the best decision you can with the information you have. If, in considering your needs and your family's lifestyle, there are elements of the application that do not fit your spec, consider these shortcomings closely. Do not hesitate to reject the application/match if you do not feel it fits your most important criteria. You are choosing to live with this individual for 12 months. Optimize as many of the elements as you can in finding your best match.

The director of one of the agencies recently told me, when discussing matching:

"We have one family who has been with us for about eight years, since the organization's inception. The host mother is very demanding during the matching process and is very specific about the characteristics she is wanting to optimize. On one hand, we consider her a bit of a nuisance during those few weeks, but, when I have thought about it afterward, I realized this family has had a successful match every time. We never hear from this family again during the course of the year. Something this host mother is doing is clearly working for her family. Ultimately, this is the true measure of success and it's clearly worth the work this woman puts into it." — Au Pair Agency

Trust your instincts with first impressions. This is your family and your children you are looking out for. Nobody knows them as well as you do. This is not a place to compromise or give "the benefit of the doubt." If something tells you this is not the right candidate for your family, reject the application and keep looking for someone closer to your spec.

"Sometimes the care and creativity the candidate has put into their application is a good indicator of their interest and enthusiasm for the adventure they are embarking upon." — Host Parent

Requesting Additional Candidates

You may decide that you do not want to pursue any of the candidates whose applications you are sent. It is clearly your right to request additional profiles. Talk this through with your local coordinator, being as specific as you can about why you are not satisfied with the selection you have been given. The coordinator can then intervene on your behalf with the agency to get applications that are more suited to your needs. The better the identification process, the less the likelihood that you will have to seek additional applicants.

Exclusivity Time Window

Most agencies give a host family 24 to 48 hours of "exclusive" time with the candidates being considered. Get busy and take advantage of this time with a first contact and possibly even a second call within the "exclusive" time period before other families also start calling the same candidates.

Phone Interviews

First Phone Call

Having read through the applications, you are now ready to conduct your first phone interviews. If the candidate is not there, explain that you are calling from America and ask if there is another number where the candidate can be reached or when would be a better time to call. If you are successful in reaching the candidate, start by introducing yourself, explaining where you are from in the U.S. (what city on a map of the U.S. is your town closest to), and briefly describing how you would like to conduct this first phone call.

Since the candidate has no advance warning of who you are or even that you will be calling today relating to an application she likely completed weeks ago, take the lead in this first phone call by asking her questions that arose in reviewing her application. You will also want to ask any of the specific questions your agency suggests in its literature, as well as some of the "tough questions" from page 38.

Take some time to describe your family, and your particular circumstances, emphasizing the points you feel are particularly important for each candidate to think about (between this first and any subsequent calls) relative to their interest in your family. End the call by asking if the candidate has any questions at this point. Keep in mind that you have just given her a lot of information that she is only beginning to think about. She may not have many questions at this point. That is OK. If you are still interested in pursuing this candidate, arrange a good time (soon, within a day or two) to call again. By then, the candidate will have absorbed and internalized much of what was said in the first call and will likely have many more questions for you. Keep in mind an au pair's language challenges.

"The au pair candidates are asked in their applications to specify what type of community and even what U.S. geographic location they are most interested in. Be mindful of the choices noted and understand whether they are flexible or if there are specific reasons why the candidate is seeking placement in California, when you may be located in New York State." — Host Parent

Clarify Your Family Circumstances

In our family's current circumstance (two middle school/high schoolers), I find that I must emphasize in the first call that I do not have babies or toddlers, that my children are in school all day, and that the au pair is more like a big sister to them. This also means that our au pair spends much of each weekday on her own and must be independent, a self-starter, with hobbies and interests to actively pursue in her spare time. Keep in mind that some au pair candidates have a distinct image of a year playing with toddlers. Our family's needs are nothing like that at this stage. Therefore, I must quickly get to the point to ensure that candidates understand this before deciding whether they want to explore further with this family of teenagers. It is much better that the au pair "self-select" herself out of my candidate pool now than later, once in the U.S. with a family whose circumstances are not what she had in mind.

Finally, be clear about the arrival date you have agreed to with the agency and be sure it corresponds with the candidate's understanding of her availability.

Second Phone Call

Decide which candidates you want to call again. The second calls are generally much more revealing. The au pair is expecting your call and has had time to think about your first conversation, talk it over with family and friends, and imagine herself in the circumstances you have described. Start by asking her how she is feeling about your first discussion. Have any questions come up that the she would like to ask or are there things that need more explanation? The candidate's reactions in this second phone call will give you a better sense of what she finds important in considering your family. After she has exhausted her immediate questions, ask any additional questions that have arisen for you and then spend time describing in more detail a typical day and week in your household. Begin to explore with candidate what type of coursework she would be interested in pursuing while in the U.S. You will be able to help formulate these thoughts into action when/if she becomes a successful candidate.

"We have had circumstances where the candidate has politely told us in the second phone call that they would prefer to continue to speak with other families about other opportunities (whether it is our geographic location or the age of our children or any other detail that might not have clicked for them in thinking further about our first conversation). Understand it is much better that you be clear in your needs, that the candidate understand these specifics and self-selects out rather than continue in a selection process that does not match their expectations and comfort level for match."
— Host Parent

Keep in mind — you have had the opportunity to see the au pair's application but they have seen nothing yet in writing on you or your family. All that they know about you is what you are telling them in these phone calls. Draw on the things you wrote in your family application and your family essay. When you do decide on a candidate, they will find significant comfort in seeing your application/family essay and feeling that it tracks well with things you mentioned in the phone conversations you have had.

Third Phone Call

After narrowing down your selection, you may want to make a third call before you make your decision. At this point it is a good idea to introduce your spouse into the interviewing to get another opinion and impression, as well as to give the candidate an opportunity to "meet" another member of the family.

This call will likely be shorter that the others but handled in much the same way as the second call — letting the candidate raise questions, then following with your additional points.

Are You Feeling Comfortable with the Candidate?

At the end of this conversation, you should be ready to ask your "candidate of choice" if she would feel comfortable joining your family for a year. If things have proceeded as they should, the candidate will feel as comfortable saying yes to you as you do in offering the position. Once agreed, you can end the conversation by telling the candidate that she should be hearing from the agency directly about further details. Inform your local coordinator immediately of your choice and ask that she or he immediately make the agency aware of the selection so that plans can be formalized for the au pair's timely arrival.

Even in the best of circumstances, getting your chosen au pair your application/essay materials through the agency takes nearly two weeks. If fax or email is available to the candidate (e.g., a parent's office fax or email), it can work well for you to fax or email the descriptive portions of your materials right away. Having this information in hand gives yet another level of comfort to the au pair and her family about the decision and her upcoming U.S. exchange.

Taping the Interview

You may want to tape your phone interviews to be able to play them back later or to share them with your spouse. Many message machines are equipped with a record feature that could be used for this purpose. If you choose to do this, you must (for legal reasons) ask the candidate if it is OK to tape your conversation. Explain your reasons for doing this and proceed if you have her permission, which you should have her repeat verbally at the beginning of the recording.

Talking to the Parents

Before you end this "selection" conversation, you may want to ask the candidate if her parents would like to speak with you briefly. The candidate may choose not to take you up on this offer, but, depending on the support from the parents on this exchange in general, a direct conversation with them may allay concerns and build worthwhile bonds that will help the overall relationship short and longer term. The media's representation of the U.S. internationally has bred a pervading impression of danger and violence. Your speaking directly with the candidate's parents can alleviate some of those general fears and give them a sense of connectedness with you and a comfort in "sharing" their daughter with you for a year.

A friend who has had three successful matches in a row even goes so far as to write one to three letters to the parents during the year, thanking them again for sharing their daughter and giving them a brief perspective of how things are going, sometimes even sharing an amusing anecdote about their time together.

Making the Selection

Be sure that all relevant parties are informed about your decision in a timely fashion — the local coordinator, the agency, any other candidates you had been talking with (the agency can handle these "close-outs"), your family, and your current caregiver.

If you have had previous au pairs, possibly even from the same home country as your current selection, you might consider giving your new au pair their names and contact numbers for an additional reference on your behalf. Especially if the two au pairs are in the same country, the advantage of the two of them talking in their native language is meaningful. This can also work if you have a close family friend who lives in the au pair's home country. Be selective about when you think this type of offer would be appropriate. It is not necessary but it can be helpful.

Completing this selection process effectively increases the probability of success in Au Pairing Up. And now that you have selected your au pair, it's time to go on to Part Four: Preparing for Your Au Pair.

PART FOUR: Preparing for Your Au Pair

Once the selection process has been completed, here are some things you can do to make the match between your family and your au pair as fruitful as possible.

The Prearrival Preparation Process

Prearrival preparation involves everyone not just you, or you and your spouse. It involves the au pair, you, your spouse, your children, and important outsiders (school administrators, friends, parents of your children's friends, teachers, grandparents, etc.) Their preparation and support of important outsiders can help, while lack of it can hurt. You may wish to create an announcement such as the following and send it to your "important outsiders." To do this, see "Au Pair Announcement Template" on the CD-ROM.)

Keep in Touch with the Candidate

Once the au pair has received your application materials, call again to keep building the relationship. Send local maps of your area, tourist brochures, and so on to your au pair to provide a sense of the "look and feel" of your general area. These are meaningful items for the au pair to share with her friends and family as the time draws near for her departure.

Within two weeks of your au pair's departure from home, call and talk about what the current weather and the varying seasons will be like in your area. This will help clarify clothing and other items to be packed. Suggest that she bring photos and easily-packed memorabilia from home to put up in her room. She may want to bring some family or special holiday recipes to share with you.

Opportunities for Your Au Pair

Watch for local adult education brochures, local community college programs, art classes, sports club programs, and the weekly newspaper "calendar" section about things to do in the area. Collect these pieces and put them aside to give to your au pair upon arrival. All of these items will be of interest as she adapts to her new life in the U.S.

Prescheduling Issues

Think about the year's schedule of family vacations, grandparent visits, holiday traditions, etc., in terms of the au pair's participation in these events. Anticipate early when you expect the au pair to take her vacation time during the year. Inform her of this and any changes that may arise as early as possible so she can start thinking about it and making plans. This information should be integrated into your "Year at a Glance" chart, page 94.

Getting the Au Pair to Your Home

Your contact with the agency will not generally be all that significant during this time. If your au pair is arriving to an orientation city first and then will travel on to your home, you will be given instructions to make travel arrangements from the orientation city to your home. The agency will leave it up to you to choose a mode of transportation and pay for the related cost. I have generally expected that the au pair is anxious to get settled and has heavy luggage to manage and have thus typically arranged for an airplane ticket. In other circumstances, train or bus transportation can work adequately also. Again, the agency will rely on you for this decision, and related costs will likewise be your responsibility.

Preparation: Your Children

If you are hosting an au pair for the first time in your family, depending on the age of your children, you will certainly want to talk about and anticipate their arrival with your entire family. With school age children, be quite specific about who is arriving (share the pictures from their application), when they are expected, where they will sleep and what the children can and should expect. Involve the children in conversation about where the au pair is from, find it on the map/globe, get storybooks from the library about the au pair's home country. In general, get the children comfortable with the fact that the au pair is coming to join the family. You will find some au pairs will respond in kind to your continued contact pre-arrival and will themselves take the initiative to write to your children while preparing to leave their home country.

Preparation: Important Outsiders

Many other people and groups, such as your friends, parents of your children's friends, teachers, grandparents, etc. will be interacting with your new au pair. Their preparation and support can help, while lack of it can hurt. Especially with pre-school and grammar school age children, introducing a new caregiver into the family is an event to anticipate with not only the immediate family, but also with teachers and close friends. As arrival date approaches, mention that your au pair will be joining you soon and solicit help from these important people to make the transition as seamless as possible for the au pair and for your children. An "Au Pair Pre-Announcement" may help this process along, by involving other friends and family members.

Au Pair Arrival Announcement

This letter of announcement is on the CD-ROM, so that you can easily customize, print, and deliver it.

Dear (friends, relatives, teachers):

On _____, our new au pair is going to arrive. Her name is _____, she is _____ years old, and she hails from _____.

We are excited about this new cross-cultural adventure, and we hope that you'll help us help her to feel at home, when you next see our children.

Best regards,

"Although I was still jet-lagged when I arrived to my host family, my host parents had the youngest child take me on a quick tour of the house. It was such a nice surprise when we got to my bedroom to see the artwork Julia had taped on my bedroom door for my arrival. It gave us both something to immediately share and talk about." — Au Pair

Preparation: More Things for You to Do

During the "lull" between the end of the application and selection process and the actual arrival of your au pair, there is much work you can do to insure the success of your new childcare solution. This work, especially including the creation of your "Standard Operating Procedure" manual and other materials, is detailed in Part Five.

One issue — driving — is so important that it is well worthwhile to consider your "policies" in advance. Preparing your "Automobile Policy" now, and organizing maps and directions beforehand will clear time for more important post-arrival tasks: like the driving lessons themselves!

AUTOMOBILE POLICY

Every family's circumstances are somewhat different relative to car use, car availability, public transportation accessibility, etc. In the suburban location where we live, one cannot get anywhere without the use of an automobile. There is virtually no public transportation within reasonable walking distance of our home and the children must be driven daily by car to school, to all of their extracurricular activities and to visit their friends.

In our circumstances, with both my husband and I working outside of our home (and having to drive individually to work each day), we must have a third vehicle available for the au pair's use with the children, for errands and, with our permission, for the au pair's personal use within the limitations we have established.

The situation for each family will differ. You must decide for yourselves how this will work for you and your au pair. If the au pair has pre-school children at home, you may not need a car available at home during the day. In this case, you must decide how you want to set limits relative to the au pair's personal use of your vehicle when you are at home.

Again, if you are in a suburban or rural location, I do feel it is very important that you have an automobile available for the au pair's use within whatever limitations you set. Remember, that generally a "busy au pair is a happy au pair." This includes being able to attend classes locally and getting out with friends in their spare time.

In our case, because the closest multi-cinema and shopping mall are at least 18 miles from our home, the car usage guidelines we have set are these:

(1) Using the car for personal use is a privilege, a big responsibility and expensive. The au pair must ask permission to use the car each time. We want to know where the au pair is going and when she expects to return;

(2) We expect the au pair to rotate the use of cars with other friends and au pairs with whom she goes out, so that everyone is carrying an equal load relative to car usage;

(3) We have set a limit of 25 miles radius that we consider "local" driving where we expect to pay for gasoline. The au pair should use common sense in combining/coordinating trips locally to minimize "back and forth" in the same day, avoiding unnecessary mileage in the process. Remind the au pair that with all expenses included as well as the wear and tear on the car, each mile of use costs about 31 cents — so a trip to the mall and back, in our situation, costs our family about $11.00 each trip;

(4) Going beyond this 25 mile radius should be rare, requires "special " permission, and requires that the au pair contribute from their own money for gasoline/parking/any parking tickets they might get, etc. These longer distance trips are unusual circumstances and should only occur 1 time per month at the most;

(5) When the au pair is out and using the car for personal use, we have an understanding that we may ask the au pair to also do an occasional errand for us as well (e.g., do an errand for me while at the mall; drop a child off at a friend's house on the way, etc.);

(6) There is good commuter rail service from a neighboring town to the metropolitan city 35 miles from us. If the au pair wants to go into the city, they should plan to take the train from the local station. Driving into the city is unnecessary and a risk we do not wish the au pair to take. Coordinating visits to the city with the train schedule takes some planning, but it is well worth the ease and convenience and avoids the risks inherent in using the family vehicle for such a trip.

(7) If the au pair should have a car accident, in the glove compartment there is a typed list of the Important Questions to ask and write down the answers for, as well as the vehicle's registration card, which includes the name and contact numbers for our insurance company.   Per the organization's policy, we tell the au pair that she is responsible for the first $500.00 worth of damages in the event of a car accident.

Once again, getting your automobile policy thought out in advance will facilitate your creation of this crucial part of the SOP.   And once your au pair arrives, you will be busy with the actual driving lessons and direction-giving. So work on this now, and, as a general guideline, think about au pair automobile issues as you would with your own 16+ year child using the family car.

"I can't drive yet, but it's really nice to have the option of seeing my friends without having to get a ride from my parents. Also, I can avoid carpooling to school, because the au pair can take me." — Host Teen

Getting Around: Maps and Directions

Now is also a good time to start writing down detailed directions to all the typical places you will need the au pair to be able to drive to.

In our home, we have a file folder in a kitchen drawer which is full of detailed written directions to the grocery store, the tennis club, the mall, the pediatrician, the hospital, the cinemas, the homes of our children's friends, the workplace for myself and my husband, the airport, other schools where our children have sports competitions, etc. This file will be invaluable in the early months of your au pair's arrival when she / he is having to find all these places on their own.

Also have a good street map of your town and the surrounding area. Go over this together the first few times you drive together so the au pair gets a sense of the area and begins to visualize where various other destinations are relative to your home. Encourage the au pair to gradually expand the regular point to point driving they do to become better acquainted with how the various towns and roads link together.

Remember that many of the destinations remain the same but au pairs change — make this transition easier on yourself by documenting standard items in writing.

Au Pair Overlap

If you have a current au pair whose term with you is ending, you may want to consider a few days (two to four days maximum) of overlap, during which your existing au pair can introduce the new au pair to your area, to her acquaintances locally, and to your family and home. If you have had a good experience with your current au pair, the overlap can be quite helpful. If however, there are some habits you would rather not share with the new au pair, you may want to start out totally fresh and take full responsibility for the orientation. This will be more work for you, but in certain circumstances it may be better to start out anew with no learned/observed "bad habits." If you are considering an overlap, be sure to discuss it with your existing au pair to clarify her roll in this changeover.

Especially at a young age, I suggest you do not start talking with your child/children about a new au pair until one to two weeks before the au pair comes to your home. Such changes are somewhat difficult for children and it is best to raise the issue when the actual arrival is immanent in order to minimize possible anxiety.

If you are planning an overlap, your current au pair should be prepared to vacate her bedroom prior to the new au pair's arrival. It should be clean and empty so that the new au pair can settle in comfortably on arrival. I know that asking your current au pair to vacate her room can feel a bit awkward, but believe me, it is critical. Your existing au pair will understand, and your new au pair will appreciate the opportunity to unpack and begin to settle in to the new surroundings. As one host mother put it, on the occasion of her first changeover/overlap, from first au pair to second au pair:

"It felt very awkward at first for me to ask our current au pair to plan to move out of her room so the arriving au pair could move in. It was exactly the right thing to do — our current au pair completely understood and our arriving au pair really appreciated being able to immediately move into her own space and start to get settled." — Host Parent

If you plan ahead with your departing au pair, you both can host an informal ice-cream social/coffee klatch during this overlap period, for the friends of your existing au pair. It is a nice gathering to say farewell to your current au pair and provides an opportunity to introduce your new au pair to the existing circle of local acquaintances.

Some of the agencies take a specific position in favor of or against an overlap of two au pairs. Know what your preference is and talk it through with your local coordinator. If you explain your reasoning, the local coordinator will likely be supportive of your position.

Post-Arrival Checklist

Having an organized checklist will help you remember what needs to be done after your au pair arrives. A customizable version of this checklist is on the CD-ROM. You may wish to review it and add to it as you await your au pair's arrival. If you like, you can use the template on the CD-ROM to do a "find and replace," replacing the words "au pair" with the au pair's name. Then you and the au pair can work on the list together, crossing off tasks as you accomplish them. Many of these items will be discussed in Part Five.

_____Introduce au pair to neighbors and child's/children's friends and their parents

_____Introduce au pair to child's/children's teachers

_____Get au pair to YMCA, tennis

_____Show au pair how to use all appliances, phones, computer

_____Show au pair how to use the phone, and where the emergency phone list is

_____Introduce au pair to other au pairs

_____Begin driving lessons, and get au pair oriented to the neighborhood

_____Introduce the SOP to the au pair, and give her a copy

_____Set up the weekly schedule, and review it at the end of each week

_____Discuss how we both feel things are going — things that are going well, and things that need to improve

_____House account notebook/recordkeeping

PART FIVE:
The "Standard Operating Procedure" Manual, or "SOP"

"Franchising" Your Au Pair

Why do McDonald's or Subway restaurants tend to have a better track record than the independent restaurant that your cousin started, then closed? Because they are franchises. In a franchised business, a Standard Operating Procedure (or SOP) manual tells the employees exactly what to do, and how and when to do it. In fact, most well-organized businesses have SOP's to help new employees adjust to the "corporate culture" of that business, in addition to knowing the tasks expected of them.

By creating an SOP for your au pair, you let her know exactly what is expected, and how to do it. A good SOP takes a lot of the work out of training an au pair. And if you plan to continue using au pairs, a good SOP provides you with a perfect training manual for your next one.

The Liebermann Family SOP, the SOP Template, and Your SOP

Over the years, and through consultation with other au pair families, I've created the "Liebermann Family Au Pair SOP." Especially for use with this book, I've also created an "SOP Template" that'll allow you to create your own family's SOP in the easiest way possible!

Here's how to do it: You can study the SOP Template in the book, start up the included CD-ROM, and enter your own choice of information into the appropriate SOP Template for your computer system. You may also wish to look at the Liebermann SOP, which is also on the CD.

Instructions and Format of the SOP Templates on the CD-ROM

For ease of use, we have included copies of the SOP Template in the formats of a number of the nation's most popular word processing programs. This way, you won't need to customize your own SOP while using software that is not familiar. For those few readers who do not have a compatible word processing program, we have included some "generic" versions which can be used with the included software.

Included on the CD-ROM are a complete set of instructions on how to use the CD-ROM. These instructions include sections on finding your way around the CD-ROM, and how to print and customize the "Standard Operating Procedure" Manual, and the additional charts. There are even basic help sections for novice users of both IBM-PC and Macintosh style computers!

There are two main strategies for customizing your SOP. Some of you (especially those with larger computer monitors) will want to keep *two* windows from the CD-ROM open. These will be the word processing window (in which you'll be customizing your SOP) and a window that shows the text of Part Five of this book (which offers suggestions and comments on the issues involved in customizing each part of the SOP). Others of you will only want to keep the word processing window open, and look at the suggestions about the SOP in the following pages of this actual book. Do what is easier for you!

Customization Issues

Even with the use of the SOP Template, you'll have to do some work, both mental (deciding upon your own rules and guidelines) and physical (entering the information into the template).

For example, your SOP will be more personal if you use a "find/replace" command to find and replace the words "(child's name)" with your own child's name! And you will need to read the instructions about each issue, decide how your family wants to handle tv watching, or non-job car use, or au pair guest visits, and insert that information into the SOP Template.

However, writing an SOP from scratch would still be dozens of times harder, and you might easily miss some of those important but not obvious issues that took me "half a dozen au pair years" to figure out!

If You Don't Have a Computer

I believe that an SOP is such an important tool for au pair hosts that even if you do not have a computer, it will be worth your while to do the following:

- Study this section of the book
- Think about the instructions, and write longhand notes to "fill in the blanks" in the different parts of the SOP Template
- Find a friend with a computer, or hire someone for a few hours to use the CD-ROM and insert your longhand notes into the SOP Template.

Doing this will save you much more time and money (and sweat and brain cells) than it will cost to pay a friend or a computer rental place (most copy shops have computer services, now) to create a good SOP for you!

What's in the SOP?

The titles and subjects you will want to address in your SOP follow this outline. Naturally, you may add or delete topics to fit the reality of your family needs. However, I (and those with whom I've shared my SOP's) have found that the following subjects are appropriate for most families. The SOP covers six main topic areas: General, About Each Child, School and After School, House Matters, The Car, and Personal (On Your Own).

General

The Introduction

Top Three Priorities in your Family (for the au pair)

Goals for the Children (from family essay)

Au pair Relationships with the Children

    Showing Affection

    Touching/Physical

Discipline

Being Consistent on Discipline

Keeping Current on Requests, and Your Best Answer

Types of Discipline

When the Child/Children Ask for Something

Common Sense/Politeness

Taking Risks: When in Doubt, Don't!

Driving Risks

Leaving the Child/Children Alone

When to Call Parents

In an Emergency or Serious Situation

If It Is Not Serious or an Emergency

General Information (Daily Schedule)

About Each Child

Personality (from family essay)

Safety Issues for Each Child

Interests Outside of School

School and After School

School, Dress, and Sports

About School

Dressing for School, Dressing for the Weather

Sports

After School

Lessons or Other After School Activities

Snacks After School

Questions about the Day

Remembering Backpacks, Clothing, Books, etc.

Important School Papers, Remembering Stuff to Be Brought Home

Homework
 After Homework Is Done

Phone and Friends, Computer and TV Use
 Phone Use
 Visits (having friends over, going to friends' house)
 Reciprocity
 Future Plans with Friends
 Computer/Internet
 Television

Summary: With the Children

House Matters

 Everything in Its Place
 Cash/House Account
 House Account Expenses

Weights, Measures, and Currency

Meals
 Snacks
 Hot Meals
 Meals Outside the Home
 Breakfast
 Dinners (together once a week)

House Maintenance
 Appliances
 Mail and Deliveries

About the Phone
 How to Answer
 Phone Messages
 Call Waiting

Phone: Your Personal Use
 Local Calls
 Long Distance Calls
 Limits on Phone Time

Driving in the Car

 Most Important! Safety First!
 Taking Care of the Car

Car Use Guidelines
 Personal Use
 Rotating Use of Cars with Other Friends
 How Far to Go, Personal Car Use, Cities

Automobile Accidents

Maps and Places to Become Familiar With

Personal: On Your Own

 Keep Us Informed
 Evenings
 Weekends
 TV
 Computer/Internet/Fax/Copier
 Your Room
 Checking In
 Personal Expenses
 Payday
 Alcohol, Cigarettes, and Drugs
 Vacation Time
 Visitors, Friends, Boyfriend

Summary

Revising Your SOP

The SOP is a document that should evolve over time. You should review and change it if necessary during your au pair's stay. Of course, you will also want to change it annually in anticipation of a new au pair's arrival, taking into account, with your edits, all the ways the children's needs and yours, as a family, change year to year. You will find some items become less important and others need more emphasis. Having a generic template on the CD-ROM makes it easy to do this. Now it's time to start learning how to use it!

The Standard Operating Procedure Template

From here on, the SOP will appear as it does on the CD-ROM. As you can see, instructions are placed in parentheses and an easily identifiable typeface above each section of the SOP. These instructions will help you craft your customized version of the SOP.

There are additional instructions placed directly on the CD-ROM to help you work on customizing your SOP and other charts and forms. Once again, all the instructions that you need to use this template, from customizing issues to basic computer skills, are right on the CD-ROM itself.

(This version of the SOP has been formatted to help you create your own customized SOP by filling in the blanks. Our comments, centered, in parentheses, and in this typeface, will help you to decide what to include. These sections should not print out in the final document , but this may depend on the word processing software that you are using. If necessary, simply delete these instructional sections.

When you have completed your personalized SOP, simply print it out. The entire SOP or any section of it can be changed easily, so you can revise parts of it as necessary. For instance, as your au pair gets more familiar with your family, with the neighborhood, and with your needs, you may want to give her more independence in her decision-making about meals or activities. On the other hand, if issues around chores, privacy, or driving arise, you can easily make changes in the SOP to clarify "the rules")

The Introduction

(In this first section of the SOP you will welcome the au pair into your family and tell her how to use the SOP. Add your family name and the au pair's name to the document in the first line!)

The (your family) Welcomes (au pair) to (your street or town)!

Welcome! We are excited that you will be joining our family! We want to make your year in the United States as easy and enjoyable as possible. We understand that many things in the US are different for you. This "Standard Operating Procedure" or "SOP" will help you to understand how we live, and what you need to know.

The SOP covers everything from emergency phone numbers to where to buy vegetables, plus a lot more. Having all of this information written down in one place will make it easier for you to know what we expect.

Important: If there are things that you do not understand in this SOP, please ask us about them! We will be glad to explain whatever you need to know! We know that this SOP contains a LOT of information. We do not expect you to memorize it all. That's why we have given you a copy of the SOP to keep. You can look at it any time you need to.

The Top Three Priorities in our Home

*(Clearly, priority #1 needs to be the children.
But in your home, #2 may be organizing playtime with other children; or helping you with errands.
#3 might be assisting in getting child/children ready and where they need to be, and on time.)*

Priority #1   —   The Children
Priority #2   —   _____
Priority #3   —   _____

Goals for the Children

(You should be able to paraphrase here the general child-rearing statements and philosophies you likely included in the family essay portion of your original agency application. If you are starting with a "blank slate." fill in the blanks below providing a sense of your parenting style, the type of home environment, as well as external experiences you are wanting for your child/children.)

To provide a home environment that offers _____.

To provide an opportunity at home, at school, and through activities outside of school to _____, with a strong sense of _____.

We are encouraging the children to be as independent as is sensible, given their ages.

Your Relationship with the Children

(This is a pretty standard description of the general relationship — of course you can change it if it doesn't suit your family. Your objective here is to describe the type of relationship you are seeking between your child/children and the au pair.)

We welcome you as a typical "big sister" into our family. We encourage you to join in our family activities, or to do "your own thing" during your spare time. We ask the kids to treat you like a "big sister," and we ask you to treat them like your own sister or brother.

Showing Affection

(Describe here your family's affection style, — warmer or cooler, more or less touching — to give the au pair a sense of what she will observe from you, as parents, with the children, and what your hope is in terms of responsiveness from the au pair toward your children.)

As parents, we are _____ with the children, for example _____.

We hope that you become comfortable enough to express your care for the children.

Treat the kids equally and with lots of patience and love as though they were your little brother or sister.

Touching / Physical

(What forms of touching and physical contact are used in your family? How do you want your au pair to relate physically to your children?)

Showing care and affection by friendly hugs, play wrestling, roughhousing, more formality with boys versus girls, very little touching, affectionate touching only with the six-year-old girl but not the eleven-year-old boy, etc., are some specifics you should mention relative to how you, as parents, are with your children and what your expectations are of the au pair in this regard.)

Physical touch in our family takes the form of _____ with (Child).

Physical touch in our family takes the form of_____ with (other child).

This should always and only be done appropriately given the ages of the children and your relationship with them.

Discipline

(We have found it helpful to start with a few general guidelines on this issue.)

Being Consistent on Discipline

It is very important to be consistent with discipline for the children. Watch how we treat the children and treat them similarly, that is, do what we would do when we aren't there.

Our children are good kids, and they will listen to you and respect you as the authority figure if you are firm and consistent with them. Do not do what is easiest. Like any children, they will take advantage of you if you "give in" to them, making it harder to discipline them next time. The key is to be CONSISTENT.

Try to be clear with them about what is right and wrong without being too hard on them. While they should view you as an authority figure, it is important that your relationship be warm and friendly.

Keeping Current on Requests, and Your Best Answer

We need to keep each other informed about what our responses have been to current requests so we can be consistent in supporting each other. If the children ask you something and you are unsure how to respond, your best answer is, "I will have to talk with your mom/dad about that."

Discipline the kids with love and explain things to them.

Types of Discipline — Physical Discipline?

(Be specific with the au pair about how you discipline your children and how you want to discipline them.

For example, in some cultures, spanking a child is considered appropriate for certain behavior . If you are opposed to physical discipline, explain that here and describe your method of dealing with inappropriate behaviors, such as "time outs," no TV etc.

Obviously, this section is very much specific to your family's philosophy about discipline, and specific to the ages of the children.)

We (sometimes, see below? never?) _____
discipline the children physically — no slapping, spanking, shaking, etc.

If Physical Discipline Is Acceptable and Needed

(If your family uses spanking as a consequence for certain "offenses," we feel that the parents only should be the spanker. If you decide to allow the au pair to spank, IT IS IMPERATIVE that you detail clearly the situations (e.g., running into the road) in which it is to be used. Once again, we believe that it is only the role of the parent, not the au pair, to use physical discipline on a child.)

Nonphysical Discipline Methods

(In this section of the SOP, you will need to detail the discipline methods that you do use. Describe time outs, depriving child of privileges, extra chores, making apologies, etc., for the au pair, since she may not be familiar with your discipline methods.)

When the Child/Children Ask for Something

When (child's name/children) ask for something — a treat at the grocery store, a snack before meals — use your common sense rather than do what is easiest. Sometimes (especially with things like eating snacks right before dinner) it is better for the child if you are a little bit "tougher."

Once again: if you are unsure how to respond, your best answer is "I will have to talk with your mom/dad about that."

When you're not sure, ask us!

Common Sense/Politeness

(Mention here the manner in which you are instilling common manners and basic etiquette, being mindful of the children's ages. The au pair's actions here should generally mirror and reinforce yours, again seeking consistency.)

The children must never treat each other or you disrespectfully. We appreciate your helping us reinforce good etiquette and manners with the children. Encourage them to say "please" and "thank you" regularly. Likewise, when they want to speak when someone else is talking, they should say "excuse me" and then wait their turn to speak. Encourage them to properly introduce their friends and acquaintances to you, when you are meeting them for the first time.

In general, if there are behaviors or habits you question in the children, please mention them to us so we can discuss them and resolve them together.

Taking Risks

There is only one rule about taking risks with the children.

WHEN IN DOUBT, DON'T !!!

Do not take any unnecessary risks with the children!

Driving Risks

(You may wish to add to these as you see fit. Remember that many au pairs will not be used to American cars or roads. Thus they should not use the phone, look at maps, or deal with children without stopping the car first.)

- Drive with extreme care.
- You and the child/children must always wear seat belts — it is the law.
- NEVER drink alcohol and drive.
- Always stop the car if you need to look at a map or use the car phone.
- If the child/children need attention, stop the car. Do not try to offer food, take off a child's coat, or do anything else while driving.
- If you are upset, or if the child/children are upset, you should stop the car rather than drive while you are distracted.
- Never drive faster than 55 or 60 miles per hour on a highway with the child/children no matter what the circumstance.
- It is better to be a bit late but safe than to risk an accident by speeding.

Leaving the Child/Children Alone

(Describe here what level of attention you expect the au pair to pay to the child/children in different common situations. Some examples follow but you will need to customize this section as needed. Because of age differences, you will need to do one of these for each child — simply copy the entire section, paste it into the text, and insert the appropriate instructions for another child.)

Leaving (Child) in the car alone: _____ (for example: never, or ok if you can see the child, car must be locked — don't forget the keys, or okay if car is locked in [small town] but never in [nearby city])

While in a store and elsewhere: _____.

If (Child) is outside playing in the yard:_____.

(Child) can go as far as _____ on (his/her) own, especially on his/her bike.

(Child) cannot go alone to the _____, etc.

When to Call Parents

In an Emergency or Serious Situation

Call (host mother or host father) at work whenever you need us. Someone always knows where to find us.

In the case of an emergency, an accident, or an illness, be sure to contact us right away.   Keep copies of the **Emergency Number List** wherever you might need them (near each telephone, in the car, etc.).

If It Is Not Serious or an Emergency

If it is not serious (you need to ask something, need us to pick up milk on the way home) you can always leave a message at work or _____ .

(Child/children) can call us at work when he/she must, but he/she should first try to work things out at home with you rather than calling us.

General Information (Schedule)

Mornings

On weekdays you must be dressed and upstairs/downstairs by _____ a.m. since (Child) must be up by _____ a.m.

You should be upstairs and around to keep (Child) moving and getting ready for school.

(Describe what must be done with the child in the morning, how much the child can do him/herself, how much the au pair should assist. Be as specific as possible, preferably in checklist form as follows.)

Before breakfast: _____.

Breakfast (see also "Meals" page 76): _____.

After breakfast:_____.

Brush teeth

Wash face and hands

Comb hair

Be sure all homework or notices are in (child/children)'s backpack.

(If you have children attending more than one school, you may need to copy the following section)

(Child)'s school is about a ____ minute drive from home. School starts each day promptly at _____ a.m. (Child)____ should be there by _____ a.m.

Evenings

Bedtime for (Child):
On weekdays between ___and ___p.m.

Other Repeated Chores

(These include brushing after meals or after eating candy, and washing hands before each meal, after using the bathroom, or after touching pets.)

(Child) should brush teeth after every meal and after eating candy. He/she should wash hands before each meal and after using the toilet.

About Each (Child)

(Describe here some of the unique characteristics of each of your children so your au pair gets a sense of his/her personality and begins to see them as you see them. In words, give a sense of the qualities, positive and negative, that you want the au pair to notice in each child to begin to understand what she/he should expect in each child, what things to be mindful and careful of, what things to encourage, what things to discourage.

The age of your child/children will significantly influence how your au pair will act and react with them. Copy this entire section to create an "About ____" section for each individual child. You may wish to refer to what you've written about your child in your "Family Essay," from the application section.)

(Child) is _____. (He/She) is _____.

Safety First!!!

(Child): Special Concerns

(List here the things that you, as the parent, need the au pair to be particularly mindful of on behalf of your child's safety and well being. Age, the setting of your home, and the nature of your community should influence the particular items you note here.)

Be extremely careful with (Child) in the following situations:

- Getting out of cars/boats
- Crossing streets
- Looking out for things hitting him/her, for example, a ball or a revolving door
- Falling off things
- Staying with you in stores, supermarkets, shopping malls, etc.

Specific Safety Issues

(Mention here <u>particular</u> safety situations the au pair should be especially mindful of, e.g., waiting for the school bus, being dropped off from the school bus, rollerblading, biking, taking walks, playing ball on the street.)

The children must wear bike helmets when riding their bikes. (Child) is allowed to ride to _____ on his/her own. (Child) needs an adult with him/her.

Interests Outside of School

(Here is an opportunity to help your au pair relate to your children, by interesting her in what interests them.)

(Child) has many interests, he/she enjoys _____.
The activities <u>he/she</u> is involved with outside of school are:

_____.

Good ways for you to share (Child)'s interest are:

_____.

School, Dress, and Sports

About (Child)'s School

(Note some specific things, as relevant, about your child's school that the au pair should be aware of, e.g., carpool arrangements, where your child gets dropped off and picked up for school, what to do if your child is not where he/she usually is for pickup, who to talk to for help.)

Dressing for School, Dressing for the Weather

(Give some guidance here about whether your child needs help picking out clothing and/or dressing. Mention what is appropriate and what is not appropriate for your child to wear and whether changing clothes is necessary when returning home from school, before going out to play. Some suggested general wording follows.)

We like our child/children to play outside as often as possible if it is not raining (depending on whether he/she has/have homework). Make sure he/she is dressed appropriately for the weather.

Always have the (child/children) dress appropriately (warm/cool) for the weather. It is better to layer clothing on cool days, so he/she can peel the clothing off during the day. It is also better for he/she to have warm clothing with him/her than to be underdressed all day. You are the best judge of what coats, hats, etc., are needed. If it is raining, he/she must wear raincoats — no arguments.

(Child) should wear _____ to school. In deciding what clothing to wear and dressing, _____.

Sports

(Note here the sports activities in which your child/children participate, where and when this takes place and what attendance you would expect of the au pair at these events. Involve the au pair in your children's lives as much as possible, especially at first, to give her a sense of the tempo of your lives.)

Provide a sense here of sports at school and outside of school — the general timing, the varied locations, family supports and attendance needed.

After a time, if you are attending your child's sporting events, you can give the au pair the option to come along or not, leaving it up to her. If you cannot make the event, I encourage you to ask the au pair to be there to lend support and encouragement.)

(Child) is at school during the week, from Monday through Friday. When he/she is playing team sports, he/she may have a game on _____ afternoon and on _____.

At this age, (Child) has sports _____ at school during the last period of the day. If he/she is playing a team sport, he/she will likely have one or two games during the week at "home" (his/her school) or away at another school. Pickup times will change according to game schedules during the school year. Besides school sports, (Child) also plays _____. For _____, he/she attends a practice session after school on _____ and often has a competitive match on _____. During the winter, we _____ and during the summer we _____ as a family.

After School

Try to remind (Child) when you drop him/her off at school or when you say good-bye in the morning what will be happening at the end of the school day. This will help YOU to remember and prepare for the after-school part of the day, also.

Lessons or Other After-School Activities

(Mention here any other types of after-school activities your child/children is/are involved with, and what the timing and arrangements are to get him/her there and back, e.g., music lessons, church school, dance, tutoring.)

Snacks after School

(This section may or may not be appropriate for your child or children. If it is, customize it by suggesting both acceptable and nonacceptable snacks and drinks.)

Before picking (Child) up from school in the afternoon, prepare a healthy snack and drink for him/her to have in the car.

He/she is just finishing sports most days when you pick him/her up and he/she is very hungry when he/she jumps into the car. His/her first words are often, "'I'm starving!"

A drink (list drinks that your child likes) plus a snack (list snacks) are always appreciated. Keep these after-school snacks healthy Do not offer, (list things not acceptable).

Questions about the Day

Always ask (Child) how his/her day was so he/she feels you are taking an interest in him/her. It works best if you ask something specific, e.g., How was field hockey today? Did you have a scrimmage? Did you play outside? How was Art today? What did you make? Try to ask questions that require more than a yes or no answer.

Please tell us how the child's/children's day was and anything that is new with him/her. If you sense something is bothering him/her, try to get him/her to talk about it with you, then tell us about it.

Remembering Backpacks, Clothing, Books, etc.

Help (child/children) remember to bring home any clothing he/she brought to school — clothing, backpack, books, etc. If it is hard for you to remember what he/she is bring to school, make a note. Since he/she take many of the same things each day (backpack, winter coat, etc.), this will get easier.

(You may wish to make a specific list of things to be remembered for each time of year, since winter and summer items will be different. If your au pair has trouble remembering to return with these things, you can prepare a list such as the following.)

Here is a list of clothing and other things that (Child) should remember to bring home:

_____

_____

_____

(For specific nonschool repeated events, such as music lessons, sports, etc., you may wish to use the "Repeated Event Directions" Template on the CD-ROM, or see page 95 in the book. This is a good place to list items that must be sent and returned with the child.)

Important School Papers / Remembering Stuff to Be Brought Home

Ask (Child) if he/she has any important papers to show you, for example, notes from the teacher, homework, etc. Put papers out for us to see next to the weekly schedule on the counter.

About _____ time(s) per month, a note may come home with (Child) telling us about a school day that will only be a half day because the teachers have meetings/conferences. Watch for those notes and be sure to mark them on the schedule so (Child) will be picked up on time.

Homework

(If you have school-age child/children, this is the place to establish rules for homework, i.e., all homework must be done before TV is turned on. If you wish the au pair to supervise homework, put all the details here.)

When (Child) gets home from school, he/she can _____. If there is homework to be done,_____.

Education is very important in our household, so schoolwork is a top priority.

After Homework Is Done

When homework is done, please do some fun things with (Child), such as (list fun things this child likes to do in free time). In general, enter into the (child's/children's) world as much as you can to understand him/her, communicate with him/her, enjoy and support him/her.

Phone and Friends, Computer and TV Use

Phone Use

(Detail rules for child's/children's use of the phone here.)

(Child) should not make or receive phone calls to/from friends until after homework is done.

(Child) should not be on the phone for more than _____ at a time.

Friends

(You may wish to list your child's/children's closest friends here. Also, if there are children you prefer your child/children not associate with, this is the place to mention it. Examples follow.)

(Child's) closest friend is _____. His/her parents are _____ and
_____. Their phone number is _____.

Another good friend is _____. His/her parents are _____ and
_____. Their phone number is _____.

We prefer that (Child) does not play with _____. If (Child) asks to play
with <u>him/her</u>, tell (Child) that you have to ask a parent if that is OK

Reciprocity

Help the child/children reciprocate with friends. If (Child) is invited for a movie
encourage him/her to return the invitation at another time.

When another parent does a "favor" by dropping (Child) off when you cannot, be
sure to thank that individual and try to return the favor when you can.

Future Plans with Friends (must check in with parent first)

Weekend plans or a sleepover at a friend's house must be decided by us. The child/
children know this. If he/she ask, say, "you need to ask your mom or dad for permission."
When in doubt, check it out (with us)!

Computer / Internet

(State here what general rules you have for your child/children with the computer, if he/she can use it on his/her own or need supervision, if you limit his/her time playing games/being in chat rooms with friends.)

There is a _____ computer for general use <u>(state where)</u>. It is set up with an
Internet capability also. (Child)'s use of the computer should be _____.

Television

(State here your general guidelines in terms of TV watching for your child/children. Suggestions follow.)

Be aware of the types of programs you are watching with the child/children and
especially the videos you watch with him/her. They should be appropriate for their ages.
Ratings are: "G" for general audiences, "PG" for parental guidance suggested, "PG-13" —
for parental guidance suggested for children under 13 (these are often not good for (child/
children), and "R" for restricted (our child/children) should not be seeing R-rated films or
videos).

Please be sure that the TV programs and videos the child/children watch are appropriate for his/her ages.

(This is a good place to add any other general instructions that feel appropriate to you, or to reinforce those instructions that are most important.)

In general, you are taking our place in doing things a parent would do. This means:

- Keeping the child/children safe: DO NOT TAKE RISKS!
- Being sure he/she are doing his/her homework.
- Taking turns helping out at: (state activity you need au pair's support with)
- Helping out once in a while at a special program in (Child)'s classroom.
- Being sure (child/children) eat healthy snacks and meals in general.
- Doing other things that we could do for him/her if we were available.

House Matters

Everything in Its Place

(Each household has its own desired level of neatness and organization, or lack thereof. The more clearly you can detail this to your au pair from the first week, the easier it will be. Here are a few suggested wordings, but you will have to add your own specifics.)

Please keep in mind a few things about household tidiness. Everything has a place, and if we keep up putting things back where they belong, they are easy to find when needed. The kids' toys in general should be in (state where). To keep the house neat, return toys back to the (state place for toys) and have the child/children do the same. If you keep everything in its place — scissors, drawing paper, stapler, scotch tape, emergency phone list, portable phones, clean clothes (put away), dirty clothes (in the hamper), the house will stays tidy with less work. Also, things will be where you expect them to be.

Cash / House Account

(If your au pair will need cash to pay for household items — gas, groceries, etc., — you will want to note here some points about a "house account."

Mention the types of things the au pair may need to buy and pay for from this account and how you would like her to keep track/take note of the spending of these funds.

I buy a small spiral-bound notebook and suggest that the au pair keep simple account of cash given to her for the house account and, in broad categories, note how it is spent and the balance left.

During the first few weeks after your au pair's arrival, this is an item you should go over at least weekly.)

Keep track of what money you receive from (host mother or host father) for the house account and what you spend it on.

- Discuss House Accounting dollars with (host mother) once a week.
- Review expenses for past week (how money was spent and recorded) and give (host mother) any receipts that she may need.
- Keep a good record of money that you have received or spent in a small notebook. You can use general categories for things you list in the notebook, for example:

Sept. 23	$ 6.25	dry cleaner
	$ 46.00	groceries
Sept. 24	$ 21.00	gas
Sept. 25	$ 60.00	cash from (host mother or host father)

Keep all receipts.

I will try to remember to give you money regularly, but if you run low, please ask for more cash.

House Account Expenses

(Be specific about what items are considered house account items so your au pair is clear about what you pay for and what she must buy on her own. Make each category a separate line.

If an item not covered by your list comes up and should be covered by the house account fund, tell your au pair in advance to avoid confusion.

As another option, you may want to use one of the commercially available house finance software packages and set up a bank account with an ATM/charge card for the au pair at your bank. You could then transfer reimbursements to the au pair for any house account whenever necessary. You could use this method also to transfer the au pair's weekly "pocket money."

In any case, help the au pair set up a bank account for her-self. It helps her conserve cash if you deposit some of her weekly "pocket money" directly into her account each week.)

Here are some of the things that we expect you to use house account money for:

- Groceries for the house
- Gas, and oil for general use of the car (<u>within your mileage limit — see page 81)</u>
- Car wash, vacuum periodically
- Meals out with the kids (you may wish to limit this amount, e.g., at most, ____times per week, or at most $____ per week total)
- Odds and ends we may ask you to pick up for the house
- (Child)'s weekly lessons, which need to be paid in cash.

In the next section, we will help you get used to US currency.

Weights, Measures, and Currency

(Remember, amidst the change in general surroundings and time zones, the au pair is also having to get accustomed to a totally different system of weights and measures, adjust from Centigrade to Fahrenheit, and convert everything of value from your currency to her currency. This is foreign translation squared!

All of this will take some time to get used to. Help your au pair along by trying to state facts in both standards (e.g., 32 degrees Fahrenheit is freezing and it is equal to 0 degrees centigrade; the closest grocery store is 4 miles away or about 6.5 kilometers) and stating specific quantities desired on a grocery list (1 pound of shaved turkey breast).

Your child/children may be able to help the au pair on this since metrics are being taught more broadly here in school.)

We know that you are used to the metric system. It is easier than our US system. Please ask for help in making conversions if you need it. Here is a basic list of a few metric equivalents:

Measures of Volume

1 liter	=	0.908 quart dry
1 liter	=	1.0567 quarts liquid
1 quart dry	=	1.01 liters
1 quart liquid	=	0.9463 liter
1 gallon	=	0.3785 deciliter

Weights

1 gram	=	0.03527 ounce
1 ounce	=	28.35 grams
1 kilogram	=	2.2046 pounds
1 pound	=	0.4536 kilograms

Linear Measure

1 centimeter	=	0.3937 inch
1 inch	=	2.54 centimeters
1 foot	=	3.048 decimeters
1 meter	=	39.37 inches
1 meter	=	1.0936 yards
1 yard	=	0.9144 meter
1 mile	=	1.6094 kilometers

Approximate Distances

Especially at first, we will try to describe walking or driving distances in metric terms. In general:

- a meter is just a bit longer than a yard (about 1.1 yards)
- a kilometer is a little more than half a mile (about 0.6 of a mile)
- a kilogram is a little more than two pounds (about 2.2 pounds)

Here are a few more approximate equivalents:

1 mile = about 1.5 kilometers

2 miles = just over 3 kilometers	5 miles = just over 8 kilometers
3 miles = about 5 kilometers	10 miles = about 16 kilometers
4 miles = just under 7 kilometers	20 miles = about 32 kilometers

Temperature Conversion

32 degrees F =   0 degrees C

Centigrade

-18   -10   0   10   20   30   40

```
  *      *    *      *      *
  *    *   *   *    *    *  *   *   *   *   *
  0    1 20 32 40 50 60 70 80 90 100  110
```

Fahrenheit

From F to C: Centigrade = (Fahrenheit -32) divided by 9 then multiplied by 5
Thus 50 degrees F = 50 - 32 = (18) 18/9 = (2) then multiply 2 x 5 = 10 degrees C

From C to F: Fahrenheit = Centigrade divided by 5 then multiplied by 9 then + 32

Thus 10 degrees C = 10/5 = (2) then multiply 2 x 9 = (18) then add 32 = 50 Degrees F

Currency

(Your au pair may not be familiar with the value of the dollar vis-a-vis her own currency. Foreign currency tables are often listed in major daily newspapers or The Wall Street Journal. *You can also call any local bank or look it up on the Internet. You may also want to write out a list like this.)*

US Dollars	(Your) Home Currency	US Dollars	(Your) Home Currency
$1	____	$20	____
$2	____	$30	____
$3	____	$40	____
$4	____	$50	____
$5	____	$75	____
$10	____	$100	____

In general, one _____ equals about $_____ in the US.

Food and Meals

Kids need to eat things that are good for them. So do adults! Here is some information about our family eating style. The information is broken down into sections on snacks, breakfast, lunch (at home and at school), and dinner. There is more information on where to get food, and how to cook it, in the section called "About Eating and Shopping."

(Describe here the nature of meals for your family. Are your child/children home for all their meals? Does lunch or snack need to be made at home and brought to school? Do parents often eat with child/children, or not?

What hours are considered mealtime in your home? When does your family have a "big hot meal" for the day? Do you sit down as a family for dinner at night?

What snack food do you encourage in the house for the child/children?

What "junk food" is acceptable in your house?

Make a point to understand the au pair's eating habits and encourage her to put on the grocery list things she likes to eat as well.)

Snacks

Here is a list of acceptable snacks:
(list acceptable snack type foods or vegetables your child likes, etc.)

Try to have fresh fruit around at all times. Especially in the summer, we eat: (list fruits family likes).

Please do not buy candy for the house. (Or, please keep some M & Ms, licorice, or whatever, on hand.)

Hot Meals

Kids need _____ hot meal(s) a day and this should generally be _____.

Meals Outside the Home

(State your policy on eating out with the child/children.
Is it allowed? Does the au pair need your permission?
Is it permissible to eat snacks in the car?)

Meals out with the child/children: _____ Otherwise, we should be eating home-cooked meals at home.

Please vary the child's/children's meals (breakfast, snacks, lunch, dinner) so he/she have a good variety.

Breakfast

Cereal is a good breakfast, we generally have two or three varieties. But, cereal every morning gets very boring. Give the child/children a variety, such as (state variety your child/children like).

Dinners

(Discuss your family's dinner habits here. We recommend
that you have dinner with the au pair at least once a week,
to check in and stay in touch.)

We start dinner generally between ____and _____p.m.
Dinner: (speak here to what things are preferred for your child's/children's dinner)

We like to eat dinner together at least ___ time(s) per week. As you meet more people and have things going on at night, this gets harder to do. We should keep trying because it is a good time for all of us to reconnect with each other.

House Maintenance

(Once again, this section will differ for each household.
Some common issues to delineate may be:

Daily bed making for child/children

Laundry

Dishwasher — filling, running, emptying it

Washing dishes by hand

Light cleaning — what is involved, tools available to help with this and where are they kept

Errands outside the home

Suggest the best time during the day for the au pair to do any necessary errands.

Rule of Thumb: Everything has a place. Important things such as scissors, staplers, adhesive tape, basic sewing items, etc., must be returned to their proper place for everyone's use.)

Appliances

(State here any unusual things your au pair should know about house appliances, plumbing, heat, etc. You may want to mention instructions for a dishwasher, washing machine, or any other appliance that you will be expecting the au pair to use. Remember, she may or may not be familiar with this type of appliance.)

Mail and Deliveries

(Mail is important to you and to the au pair. Tell her when and where the mail is delivered and where she should put it each day so you can find it when you return home.)

Mail is delivered (state where) every day Monday through Saturday around _____a.m./p.m. We do not receive mail on Sundays nor on most holidays. Please feel free to sort through the mail to take out your letters. Please put child's/children's mail _____(state where) and the rest of the mail, (state where). If I/we collect the mail, we will always leave yours on (state where) in your room.

Sometimes we will get special packages/overnight envelopes from FedEx or UPS and the driver may ask you to sign that you have received of these packages. Please do so and leave this mail with the rest tell us that something special has arrived.

About the Phone

(Detail your policy on phone use, message taking, use of the answering machine, etc.

It may be helpful to buy a user-friendly phone message book, with spaces for caller, number, date, and message. Show your au pair how to fill out the book.

Write out how you would like the phone to be answered. If you have call waiting or other services, explain them.

*Note also the **EMERGENCY PHONE LIST** in the "Beyond the SOP" section. Customize it, then discuss it with your au pair, and post copies in all appropriate places, including the car.)*

How to Answer

Please answer the phone when you are at home. Do not leave calls to be answered by the answering machine. Please answer the phone like this: "Hello, (host family surname)'s residence, (au pair's name) speaking. Who is calling, please?"

Phone Messages

Messages are very important, and you must take care to write them down (date, time, name and phone number). Have callers spell their names, if necessary, and repeat the spelling back to them if needed. It is important to get it right even if it takes a little more time.

Call Waiting

Please respond to "call waiting." If you hear a "beep" noise, you must press the "flash" button to talk to the person who is interrupting. Then you must press the "flash" button again to return to the first caller. This is a little bit tricky at first, so we will practice this with you.

Likewise, we know your messages are also important, and we will write notes for you when someone calls while you are out and will put them (state where).

Phone — Your Personal Use

(State any special instructions you may have about your phone and phone use. Help the au pair to tell the difference between local and long distance calls.

Almost all host families require au pair's to pay their own long distance calls. With the numerous phone cards available now, encourage your au pair to become aware of the best deal for calls to her home country. Comparative shopping on this item can bring great results.)

Local Calls

Local calls are (free, or low cost per call). The following towns are considered local calls: (mention local towns included in local area). Any calls to places farther away will be very expensive, since they are considered long distance calls, such as (mention nearby cities that are outside the local area,; often an au pair will think that because a city is nearby it will be a local call).

Long Distance Calls

You are responsible for paying for your own long distance calls (including international calls, calls outside the local calling area, and taxes on these calls). I will show you the telephone bill each month so you can add up your own calls and pay for them. Make sure you know which calls are long distance. Phone numbers with area codes of (800) or (888) are free. To get a phone number anywhere in the US, and Canada, dial 1-(the area code of the number you are seeking) - 555-1212. An operator or a computerized operator will then ask you "what city" and "what name or listing," and then will tell you the phone number.

Limits on Your Phone Time

(If you need to keep the phones free for your use in the evenings, you should specify a reasonable limit to the au pair's calls. You will also want the au pair to limit her phone use during the time she is with the children.)

We need to be able to receive and make phone calls. If you would like to be on the phone for a long call, please ask us in advance.

Also, in general, try to limit your phone calls during the hours you are at home with the kids. Use the time the (child/children) **is/are** at school to make arrangements with friends. When you are at home with (child/children), I want to be sure he/she feels you are here for him/her, playing with him/her, listening to his/her stories, helping him/her with homework, getting a snack, etc.

Driving in the Car

(This is an extremely important and individual issue that you will need to really think through. Read the following but customize it in any way you see fit. If you live in an area with good public transportation, you may want to "figure that into the equation." You may wish to be more specific, explicit, and restrictive about driving issues until the au pair is more used to driving, and has demonstrated competence. You can then change this section and print it out again — and that's the beauty of an electronic SOP!)

IMPORTANT: No matter what other rules you institute, remember to stress safe driving practices, even if they mean "getting there a little bit later.")

Remember that driving with the children — or on your own — is a big responsibility. A car is an expensive machine and must be cared for. You will mostly use the _____ (mention here car or cars the au pair will likely be using during her stay with you and any unusual things about the car/cars).

Most Important! Safety First!

Watch your speed. No place you need to be and no amount of time you are late should be an excuse for speeding in the car. It is better that you get there safely even if you arrive a little late.

Drinking alcohol and driving is an extremely serious offense in the US. Do not drink and drive. Do not get in a car as a passenger with someone who has been drinking, or whose judgment you are not confident of. Call us, we will come and get you safely home. Even if you yourself have been drinking, we will appreciate your good judgment in **calling us instead of driving** while you have been drinking.

Taking Care of the Car

Watch the gas gauge so you don't run out of gas. Use _____(state type of gas if you have preference). Whenever you stop for gas, fill the tank.

Have the oil checked occasionally (note every number of fill-ups). The oil needs to be changed every ____ miles.   Watch for this and remind us so we can schedule oil changes and general maintenance. The "Check Oil" light is very important and you must always STOP immediately at a gas station if this light goes on. This is important and should not be ignored.

Water can only be checked if the car has not been running for long. Be sure the fluid levels in the car are checked regularly (when you check the oil or have the oil changed).

Write down the mileage at every oil change; about 4000-5000 miles later it needs to have the oil changed again. Help keep us aware of this on the (car) so we can schedule and plan for service.

Keep the cars clean of papers, cups, etc.

Please be aware of the temperature gauge. Never drive if the engine is too hot. Instead, pull over and call someone. (Mention here if you have an automobile service, e.g., AAA, that the au pair should be aware of also, in case of road trouble.) Lock the car outside the house and wherever you leave it. All important registration papers, insurance papers, and questions to ask if you are ever in an accident are in the glove department.

Do not leave (child/children) alone in the car.

Always mention immediately any noises, smells, smoke, etc., that you notice driving the car so they can be fixed as soon as possible.

Take care of the car — it is there for you, us, and the child/children to get around.

Car Use Guidelines

*(Once again, these will have to be individualized
to fit your needs.)*

The car usage guidelines we have set are these:

1. Personal use

Using the car for personal use is a privilege, a big responsibility and expensive. You must ask permission each time you use the car. We want to know where you are going and when you will return.

2. Rotating use of cars with other friends

When you go out with friends, we expect them to take their turns driving their own cars so that one person is not always the driver.

3. How far/where you are allowed to drive and paying for gas

*(You may wish to set these limits to avoid "unauthorized"
travel to the nearest city.)*

We have set a limit of ____ miles radius that we consider "local" driving. We will pay for gasoline within this area, whether you are driving with or for the child/children or using the car for your own personal use. Try to plan your local trips to avoid unnecessary mileage. The cost of gas, insurance, and general wear and tear on the car amount to about 31 cents a mile. A trip to the _____ (state popular place within 15 - 20 minutes of your home and back, costs our family about $__.00.

4. Longer trips

If you want to drive beyond this _____-mile radius, you will need special permission. For such trips you must pay for gasoline, parking, any parking tickets you might get, etc. These longer distance trips are for special circumstances and should only occur once a month at the most.

5. Combining personal use with house errands

When you are using the car for personal use, we may ask you to also do an occasional errand for us as well (e.g., do an errand for me while at the mall, drop a child off at a friend's house on the way, etc.).

6. Rules about traveling to (nearest large city)

(State here how travel to the city is to be handled — driving allowed? Train? Bus? If parts of the city are not safe, these must be specified, in words, and on a map.)

Please think of borrowing our car for your own use the way you would borrow your parent's only automobile. Simply say, "I'd like to go for a workout, is it OK if I use the van?" Usually, it will be fine, but we appreciate knowing where you are going and generally when you will be back. Remember, using our car for your personal use is a privilege and a responsibility.

If you have a car accident in which you are at fault, (state the policy of the au pair organization as it relates to car accidents — deductibles, any distinguishable difference between "on duty" use verses personal use in the event of an accident, etc.)

Automobile Accidents

(Spending time orienting the au pair to driving your vehicles and the various places she will be traveling to is an important first step. Every host family hopes that there will be no vehicle accidents while the au pair is driving. On the chance that there could be an accident, it is IMPORTANT to review the basic steps to be aware of. Show the au pair what the car registration looks like, and where it is kept in your vehicles. Go over the steps noted in the following section, outlining what is to be done if there is an accident. If your insurance company has a pamphlet outlining general guidelines to follow in the event of an accident, keep one in the glove compartment. An auto accident is an upsetting event; you can help the au pair cope with her responsibilities by having these tools readily accessible to her if ever needed.)

If You Are Involved in an Automobile Accident

(This information is derived from the Driver's Manual for the Commonwealth of Massachusetts. The laws in your state may differ somewhat, but should be included here.)

When involved in a crash, regardless of how minor it seems, you must stop your car. **Never leave the scene of an accident** — it is against the law and you could be charged with "hit and run."

When involved in an accident, you should not argue with the other parties involved. It will not help the situation and could make matters worse.

If the Damage Involves Property Damage Only (no injuries to any people)

1. Move your vehicle off the road if possible.

2. Exchange name, address, driver's license number, vehicle registration, and insurance information with **all** drivers or property owners involved.

3. If you have damaged a parked vehicle or stationary property, you must try to locate the owner to report the accident or notify the local police.

4. You must complete and file an accident report with both the Registry of Motor Vehicle department and the local police department within five (5) days of the event. You must report ANY crash where there has been $1000 or more of damage to property.

5. If you have injured a cat, dog, or any other animal, notify the local police and if possible, the owner.

Accidents Involving Injuries

1. Check to see if anyone is injured.

2. Call the police and request an ambulance or rescue squad, if necessary.

3. If possible, move your vehicle off the road.

4. Exchange name, address, driver's license number, registration, and insurance information with any person injured or with **any other** driver or property owners involved.

5. You must complete and file an accident report with both the Registry of Motor Vehicle department and the local police department within five (5) days of the event. The law requires you to report ANY accident in which someone is killed or injured or where there has been $1000 or more of damage to property.

6. Notify your insurance company.

AGAIN, HAVING A CAR FOR YOUR USE IS A PRIVILEGE AND A VERY BIG RESPONSIBILITY. Use it carefully.

Maps and Places to Become Familiar With

(State here where maps and directions to most common destinations can be found. Have for general use any train, bus, or subway schedules/maps that would be useful to the au pair. See also the section on "Maps and Directions," page 83, and the chart labeled "Places to Become Familiar With," in the "Beyond the SOP" section below.)

Maps and directions are kept _____. You should also study our list of "Places to Become Familiar With" and "What to Get Where."

Personal: On Your Own

Keep Us Informed

(State here your required curfew during the week/week-ends. Be specific. Note also how you want a change of plans to be handled. If, for example, au pair is out for the evening and decides to stay overnight at a friend's, do you want a phone call about such change of plans? Be specific.)

When out on your own, we would like to know generally where you are going and when you will be home. Call us (at any hour) with plan changes. We feel responsible for your health and well-being while you are living with us as part of the family.

Always leave a note if you go out while we are gone. We will always leave a note for you, too, to tell you where we are going and how we can be reached if needed.   Leave this kind of note _____.

(State where in the house such notes should be left to be sure they are seen.)

Evenings

(State what the general on duty/off duty circumstances are for evenings, during the week, and on weekends. If evening babysitting is needed, where will this be noted and how soon in advance of the event will you generally let the au pair know?)

Weekends

(Again state the general circumstances/schedule on week-ends. If babysitting is needed, where will this be noted and how soon in advance of the event will you generally let the au pair know?)

TV

(State here the general circumstances regarding TV usage and preferences. Does a specific TV have a VCR to watch videos or have the cable or DirecTV connection? Does host father get preference for channel choice when home?)

Computer/Internet/Fax/Copier

(State here the general circumstances regarding computer, Internet, fax, and copier usage and preferences.)

These are expensive pieces of equipment and must be used properly. If you are having any difficulties, PLEASE DO NOT CHANGE ANY OF OUR ESTABLISHED CONFIGURATIONS. Instead, just mention it to either of us, so we can figure it out.

Your Room

(In this section you should consider how much autonomy the au pair will have in her own room. Obviously, it is her "sanctuary" and private spot, but you may wish to consider issues such as neatness of her room, noise in the room, eating in the room, etc.)

Checking In, When You Arrive Home at Night

(Establish a signal with your au pair to let you know she is in for the evening. Perhaps she can turn off a hallway light or the outside front door light when she comes in.)

Personal Expenses

(This seems like a fairly standard list for most au pair hosts, but you may wish to add or subtract from it.)

These are the types of items you will need to buy with your own money:

Makeup and other personal items

Videos for your own entertainment by yourself or with friends

Gas and other car expenses for personal use (trips beyond local area)

Train rides (personal) into (local metropolitan area)

Your meals out without kids

Stamps, etc.

Long distance phone calls including tax

Car insurance deductible in the event of a car accident in which you are at fault.

Payday

(Note here what day you will consider "payday" and in what form you will pay your au pair — cash, check, or direct deposit to her local bank account, if any. Keep this date "sacred". Pay Day is Pay Day — respect it.

Note here if a local bank account with ATM card access is something you suggest the au pair establish.

Your au pair may have the occasional need to write a personal check, but may not have that capability with their bank account (eg. buying a CD by mailorder). I make sure our au pair knows I can write a check for them and simply deduct this amount from their coming week's pocket money. This convenience is a kindness you can offer and is easier for the au pair than purchasing, for cash plus a fee, a money order at the local post office.)

We will pay you on _____, in the form of _____.

We will help you to establish a personal bank account.

If you want to pay for something personal with a check, let me know.

Alcohol, Cigarettes, and Drugs

(Obviously, you cannot stress the dangers of drinking and driving often enough. You should be clear that any illegal drug usage is cause for immediate termination. Your policy on tobacco will probably depend on your own use.)

Drinking alcohol and driving is a serious offense in the US. Do not drink and drive. Do not get in a car as a passenger with someone who has been drinking or who you think is not able to drive. Call us, we will come and get you safely home.

Our home and our automobiles are smoke-free. If anyone visiting needs to smoke, they must go outside the house or car.

Illegal drug use is an extremely serious offense in the US. Any use of illegal drugs will be immediate cause for termination.

Vacation Time

(Note here when you anticipate the au pair being able to take vacation, as discussed in the text. Can the two weeks be taken together, or must they be taken separately? Does the au pair anticipate family/friends coming from her home country with whom she would hope to take some vacation time? Talk this through so there are few surprises. Try to determine as early in your year as possible when this can be scheduled. This is important for the au pair's planning and for yours should you need alternative childcare arrangements in the au pair's absence.

Some au pairs will need to coordinate their vacations with others. Other au pairs will have no particular plans and will work with whatever weeks can be arranged, but may need your help in choosing a trip. The travel organizations noted in the workbook arrange student trips throughout the year at very reasonable rates.)

Visitors, Friends, Boyfriends

Local Friends (Female, Male)

(Mention here how you feel about friends staying overnight. Can you accommodate this in your home? Where should friends sleep? Do you have a "rollaway" or cot? What permission or notice would you want if it is allowed?)

Family/Friends from the Au Pair's Home Country (female, male)

(Remind the au pair that she will have responsibilities whether she has visitors or not, if she in not on vacation. Determine how you feel about having people visit from your au pair's home country. Can you accommodate this in your home? What length of stay would be acceptable, for how many persons — together or separately?

*Where should they sleep? What permission or notice would
you want if it is allowed? If there are good alternatives for
reasonably priced bed and breakfast places nearby,
you can mention that option.)*

If you are not on vacation when someone is visiting from out of town, you will still have responsibilities with the children, etc.

If You Have Questions

We understand that this SOP is a long and complicated document. If you have any questions, now or at any time, please ask us. We want to help you in any way that we can.

Summary

This whole situation works best if everyone GIVES as much as they can. Please offer to help wherever needed instead of waiting to be asked. This includes times at home as well as times at the homes of our friends, or relatives.

The Golden Rules

#1. Everyone — adults, kids, and the au pair — should work as hard as they can to make this arrangement work.

#2. Deal with things as they arise. Communicate.

The Top Three Priorities

Remember, the Top three priorities in our home are:

PRIORITY #1   —   The children
PRIORITY #2   —
PRIORITY #3   —

Remember, in terms of taking risks:

When in doubt — DON'T.

PART SIX: Beyond the SOP

In addition to the SOP, we have developed a number of convenient ways to present information to the au pair. These include daily, weekly, monthly, and yearly calendars, as well as specific task forms, a "Post-Arrival" checklist, and a few useful letters. Some of these items (such as the checklist, or the "Au Pair Arrival Announcement," have already been described at the appropriate place in this book. A few others (such as the "Letter of Support," for when the au pair leaves) will be described later.

In the following section, I will discuss some additional important charts and forms. Once you have created these, discuss them with your au pair as part of the SOP discussion.

Schedules: Customized by Computer or Hard Copy and Longhand?

Depending on the degree of your involvement with computers in daily life, the variability of your schedule, and other imponderables, there are two different ways in which you can use the four main schedule forms: Day, Week, Four Week, and Year.

Some au pair hosts may find it convenient to use the templates on the CD-ROM to create, revise, and update the schedules as needed. Others may prefer either to print out a customized blank schedule from the CD-ROM, or simply to photocopy the blank forms provided below, and then fill them in via longhand. Or you may wish to do a "hybrid" variant: create a schedule that has the main repeated events on it (school times, weekly music lessons or athletic events, etc.) then print out a number of these, and fill in the "oddball" events by hand

Schedule Forms: About the Weekly Schedule

Although perhaps not technically part of the SOP, another working document you will find extremely useful is a written schedule for the week (see a blank and a completed version below). Going over this with your new au pair is a good way to familiarize her with your general schedule.

I tend to fill in the coming week's schedule Sunday night or early Monday morning, before everyone else rises. I sit down with my own calendar, the children's school calendar, and the scheduling form. If I have a need for evening babysitting coming up, I note it on the appropriate day as soon as I know so the au pair can plan accordingly. Likewise, I encourage the au pair to note specific commitments in the future (after mentioning them to me first) for example, cluster meetings, class schedules, etc.

On the following page is an enlarged weekly schedule, oriented "the long way" to maximize its size. You may wish simply to xerox and fill in by hand the "blank" copy at the end of the book.

	Before School	School	After School	Evening
Mon.	find flute things	8 - 3	4 pm Flute Lesson see "task sheet" Pick up fresh fish <u>at Seafood, Inc.</u>	Friend Lily over for dinner <u>needs ride both ways</u>
Tues.	pack swim gear	8 - 3	6 pm Swim Team see "task sheet" Dinner out <u>before Swim</u>	Homework then right to bed
Wed.		8 - 3	You will need to be evening — rent a	with kids all day and video if you want
Thurs.		8 - 3	(daughter) has playdate with Jenny 3 - 6 pm needs ride home	Cluster meeting 7 - 9:30 pm
Fri.				
Sat.				
Sun.				

About the Daily Schedule

Some families will find that a weekly schedule has enough room to detail each day's activities. If not (especially if you have multiple children with very different daily agendas), you may wish to create a daily schedule form as well, perhaps even using a separate page for each child. You may find yourself using a form of this type only during the most hectic times, such as the day before a long out of town vacation or the day of a special event!

Daily Schedule   Date: _____

7:00 am

8:00 am

9:00 am

10:00 am

11:00 am

12:00 noon

1:00 pm

2:00 pm

3:00 pm

4:00 pm

5:00 pm

6:00 pm

7:00 pm

8:00 pm

9:00 pm

About the "Four Weeks-at-a-Glance" Form

This form, although less detailed than the Weekly version, will help to give both you and your au pair a sense of what lies ahead. You'll find two "blank" versions on pages 137 and 138 (one chart with "categories," the other without), or you can customize your own from the CD-Rom. Some families prefer the "Monthly" version, on the next page.

Week of 10/13/99	Mon	Tues	Wed	Thurs	Fri	Sat	Sun
School		NO SCHOOL			Cupcakes for all		
Shopping				Pick Up Cake			
Afterschool		piano lesson	soccer game				
Evening				Birthday Party		Parents Out late	
Other	cluster mtg 7 pm			Grandparents visiting until Sunday the 19th			

	Mon	Tues	Wed	Thurs	Fri	Sat	Sun
School							
Shopping							
Afterschool							
Evening							
Other							

	Mon	Tues	Wed	Thurs	Fri	Sat	Sun
School							
Shopping							
Afterschool							
Evening							
Other							

	Mon	Tues	Wed	Thurs	Fri	Sat	Sun
School							
Shopping							
Afterschool							
Evening							
Other							

About the "Month-at-a-Glance" Form

Probably the main use for this variation of the Four Week form is to show events that only occur once in a while, such as vacations, trips, doctor appointments, etc.

Month at a Glance   Date: July, 2003

1.
2.
3. No Flute lesson today — teacher on vacation
4. Cape Cod for the Day, home very late
5.
6.
7. Orthodontist Visit for (son)
8.
9.
10. July 10 to July 17 We will be on vacation, you will have the week off.
11.
12.
13.
14. Out of town guests coming July 14 to 16
15.
16.
17. No flute lesson today — teacher on vacation
18.
19.
20. We will be gone all day, 7 am to late, you'll need to be with kids all day
21.
22.
23.
24. Cluster Party for all area au pairs at Beach — must bring food to share
25.
26.
27.
28. Piano Tuner coming, make sure you have check to pay him
29.
30.
31.

About the "Year-at-a-Glance" Form

You may also find useful a schedule for the year (in much more general terms), noting events you expect to attend together (e.g., a play, a trip) and weeks of vacation (the au pair's and yours as a nuclear family) or work holidays. As much as possible with today's busy lives, and as soon as possible, identify times that you expect the au pair to be "on duty" as well as not. There will of course be changes from time to time, but a sense of predictability, knowing when she will be on and off duty, is appreciated by the au pair.

June   (Au Pair) arrives June 8
              School Ends June 21

July   (daughter) in swim camp 7/6 - 7/12
              family vacation 7/15 - 7/29 (au pair) is off

August   Everyone to Cape Cod 8/12 - 8-16
              (au pair's) mother visits 8/22 - 8/27

September   School starts 9/3

October

November

December   Everyone to Florida 12/17 - 12/29

January

February

March

April

May

Repeated Event or "Task" Form

Many things that you will want your au pair to do (with or without kids) are repeated events. Putting all of the information about one "event" on one sheet of paper will help a lot, especially at first. This is how I like to format such a "Task Sheet." Use the template on the CD-ROM to make up Task Sheets of your own, starting with the most common ones.

Repeated Event Directions

(Child's) Weekly Piano Lesson with Mrs. Sottovoce

Contact Information

Mrs. Cassandra Sottovoce   Phone: (XXX) XXX- XXXX

When?

Every Tuesday, must arrive by 5 pm sharp

Where? Directions: (use many short lines, not one big "chunk," lots of space)

20 Delaware Street, Ourtown

Take RIGHT out of school's circular driveway (as if heading home) but at Flair Dry Cleaner's - take left onto Rt. 97 - street between Fire Station and Henry's Market parking lot.

Follow Rt. 97 for only 1/8 mile to light (a Schoolyard and church at this intersection) and go LEFT onto Conant St..

Follow Conant St. all the way to intersection / light with Rt. 62 and take RIGHT onto Rt. 62.

Follow Rt. 62 for about 1-2 miles to Summer St. on RIGHT (new houses there and small green/garden area in middle of street at this right turn). Take RIGHT onto Summer St.

Follow Summer St. and will pass St. John's Prep. School and take 3rd RIGHT after school onto Delaware St., then 1st left (still Delaware St.).

Fourth house on left is #20 Delaware St.

How Long?

(Child) will be there 1 hour (You may leave to shop, but return before the hour is up)

What to Bring:

- $15 cash to pay the **teacher**
- All necessary music books
- Workbook sheets for review
- Snack to eat in car and drink

Phone Contact: Emergency and Otherwise

Having a clear and simple plan for emergency phone use is important, even though we all hope it will never be used. The following one page "Emergency Phone Contact List" will provide an easy to use guide for the au pair. It's on the CD-ROM, for you to customize as needed. Having a short "Script" for the au pair to use in an emergency contact situation will be especially useful if the au pair is not a native English speaker.

The other phone lists are self-explanatory. Having all of your commonly used numbers in one place will make life easier for your au pair.

EMERGENCY PHONE CONTACT LIST

(IMPORTANT: Make sure that your home is on a 911 network, then advise the au pair to call 911 first in the event of a serious problem. This will be easier than trying to call the police or fire departments, since the 911 network should be able to automatically tell where the call is coming from. Specify which parent should be called first, in an emergency to save time. Make copies for car, to put near each phone, etc. You may prefer the simpler version on page 142.)

In an emergency like a fire or a bad accident at home, call 911 first!

EMERGENCY	911
FIRE	number
POLICE	number
AMBULANCE	number
POISON	1-800-682-9211
(Pediatrician)	number
(Closest Hospital)	number

After emergency help has been called, call us.
Call 911 first.

What to say if we are at work:

"My name is _____. I am the _____'s au pair.
This is an emergency. I must talk to Mr._____ right now."

(Husband's) WORK	1-area code-number, ext.
(Husband's) CAR	1-area code-number
(Wife's) WORK	1-area code-number
(Wife's) CAR	1-area code-number

GENERAL PHONE CONTACT LIST

HOME PHONE	1-area code-number
HOME FAX	1-area code-number
(Husband's) CAR	1-area code-number
(Husband's) WORK	1-area code-number, ext.
(Husband's) Work FAX	1-area code-number
(Husband's assistant- name)	1-area code-number, ext.
(Wife's) WORK	1-area code-number
(Wife's) WORK FAX	1-area code-number
(Wife's) CAR	1-area code-number

EMERGENCY NUMBER for CAR

AAA Car Service (member #)	1-800-222-4357

INFORMATION: to get PHONE NUMBERS   1-(area code)-555-1212

OTHER FAMILY

(Maternal Grandparents)	1-area code-number
(Paternal Grandparents)	1-area code-number

(Aunt)   1-area code-number

(Uncle)   1-area code-number

NEIGHBORS

(Name)   number

(Name)   number

(Name)   number

OTHER IMPORTANT PLACES WE GO

(Children's School-name)   number

(Town Library)   number

(Church)   number

(Sports Club)   1-area code-number

(Tennis Club)   1-area code-number

(Boat Club)   number

HOUSEHOLD CONTACT PEOPLE

(Lawn, Snow Plowing—name)   number

(Heat Company—name)   number

(Plumber—name)   number

(Electrician—name)   number

(Local Variety Store)   number

(Local Pizza place)   number

(Auto Repair Shop—Car #1)   number

                         Car #2)   number

FAMILY FRIENDS

(Name)   number

(Name)   number

(Name)   1-area code-number

CHILDREN'S PHONE LIST

(Son's Friends)

Friend's name   Phone Number

Friend's Address   (names of friend's Father & Mother)

Friend's name   Phone Number

Friend's Address   (names of friend's Father & Mother)

(Son's Teachers and other Numbers)

School Teacher's name   Phone Number

Piano Teacher's Name   Phone Number

Soccer Coach's name   Phone Number

(Daughter's Friends)

Friend's name   Phone Number

Friend's Address   (names of friend's Father & Mother)

Friend's name   Phone Number

Friend's Address   (names of friend's Father & Mother)

(Daughter's Teachers and other Numbers)

School Teacher's name   Phone Number

Flute Teacher's Name   Phone Number

Swim Coach's name   Phone Number

Places to Become Familiar With

(Set this up as a checklist, listing the places/people that are important for the au pair to become familiar with and meet. Following is an example list of common items. You will want to help the au pair compare this list to the list of "What to Get Where," since many of the stores on that list will also be on this one.

NOTE: If there are areas, perhaps in nearby cities, that are not safe to drive in, these should be listed as well.)

In (local town):

_____downtown (local town)

_____local post office

_____pizza place

_____local convenience store

_____local parks

_____fire station

_____(nice route to walk/jog/bike)

In (neighboring larger town):

_____dentist

_____library

_____bank

_____playgrounds, soccer fields, tennis courts

_____train, bus, subway station (to metropolitan city)

_____local grocery store

_____fish store

_____hardware store

_____child's/children's friends homes

_____nearest highway

In (neighboring small city),

_____downtown

_____larger hardware store

_____super-sized supermarket

_____large multiproduct general store
_____large drug store (for all prescription drugs and toiletries)
_____specialty food store
_____YMCA
_____local parks,
_____local beaches

In (town where child/children attend school):
_____school
_____larger YMCA
_____pediatrician's office (kids' doctor)
_____local hospital
_____tennis club
_____other train stations
_____local cinema

In (another neighboring small city):
_____museums
_____downtown shopping area

In (another neighboring city):
_____cinemas
_____shopping malls
_____sports equipment stores
_____(child's/children's) orthodontist)
_____car dealership/service center

In (another city):
_____(host father's work)

In (closest metropolitan city):
_____by train;
_____airport by car

In another city
_____(host mother's work)

About Eating and Shopping

(These forms will help your au pair to shop and to prepare meals. You may want to put all of the recipes that you would like her to use in one spot, or mark your cookbooks with "Post-It™" notes so these recipes are easy to find.)

Recipe List for Family Dinners

These are classified as **E = Easy, or H = Harder.**

Harder means more time required with marinade, layering a casserole, must be prepared then cooks for awhile on stove top etc.

The information in (parentheses) tells you where to find the recipe. I have also written down what to add to the main part of the meal, such as rice, salad, etc.

1. H   Chicken Dijon (in cookbook "Joy of Chicken," page __). This recipe is good with rice or mashed potatoes plus vegetable / salad.

2. E   Beef Mititei (filed under "Beef" in recipe box) — use ground Turkey instead of Beef sometimes, plus potato plus vegetable / salad.

3. H   Artichoke Pasta (Pasta — recipe on side of pasta box) or any other type of Pasta with Sauce plus Salad.

4. H   Cheese Strata (in recipe box) plus Salad.

5. E   Beef Burritos (use Burrito dinner "kit" and add ground beef and chopped tomatoes, lettuce, mozzarella cheese, onions, pineapple). Use ground Turkey instead of Beef sometimes.

When Just with the KIDS

1. E   Macaroni and cheese plus green vegetable plus Salad.

2. E   Beef or Turkey Hot dogs and Boston Baked Beans (can or jar) plus Salad.

3. H   Homemade Pizza — make this on store bought Pizza dough or on Pita bread rounds cut open into two sides or on English muffins cut open into two sides (Doing pizza is fun to do with the kids as a dinner project where the varied things they can put on their individualized pizzas are each in separate bowls so they can each create their own with the things they like, doing their initial in grated cheese, etc.).

4. E   Fish sticks (come frozen in box) plus Salad plus Vegetable.

5. E   Kielbasa with barbecue sauce plus two vegetables.

Vegetables Everyone Likes

Buy Fresh or Frozen (try not to get canned veggies)

Green/Yellow/Orange Veggies — can do more than one at a meal

Carrots (baby carrots are best, even good raw)

Broccoli (especially w/ melted cheddar cheese)

Cauliflower (w/ melted cheese or w/ browned bread crumbs)

Chinese Pea Pods — quick stir fried

SALAD — mixed green , Caesar, Cucumbers with Yogurt dressing

Squash — Zucchini (yellow or green), butternut squash, acorn squash

Green Beans   (good recipe with canned tomatoes in recipe box); French Green Beans cooked at the end in buttered & browned bread crumbs

Starch type Vegetables (only 1 per meal)

Potatoes — done almost any way (especially mashed or Boiled)

Rice (once in a while — especially flavored rices / Rice-A-Roni)

Noodles / Pasta

Corn   Peas

Mixed Vegetables & Pasta (comes in frozen bags)

"Where to Get What" Shopping Chart

(Your au pair, especially if she is from an Eastern or Southern European country, may not be familiar with the vast array of consumer goods and services available to your family. This type of chart will help her to shop.)

Food, Groceries

Big Grocery Shopping — at Large SUPERMarket in neighboring town

A few key items — to smaller supermarket in bordering town

Milk, missing basics — local convenience store in our town

Meat for special occasions — specialty butcher shop in bordering town

Fish — Fish shop in bordering town

Toiletries, Prescription Drugs, Gas, Videos, Hardware, etc.

Toiletries and Drugs — CVS in bordering town. Pharmacist has our insurance drug card on file for any doctor's prescription.

Otherwise any CVS, Walgreen's and even grocery stores carry basic toiletries.

Gasoline — cheaper to pump yourself. Sometimes particular stations running a special in winter for ski passes, in which case we should all try to frequent that brand to get the coupons.

Oil change / Car repairs — we tend to bring each vehicle to the dealer where we bought it.

Post Office — Every town has one. The most convenient and closest is in our own town.

Videos — neighboring town's Blockbuster or our town's convenience store. membership card or number?

Dry Cleaning — most convenient is the one on the way to children's school. Easy to drop off and pick up there after dropping the children off at school.

Hardware Store — Biggest one close by in bordering city. Smaller one with less selection in bordering town.

Seamstress — in same town as children's school.

Kitchen tools and items — Kitchen store near BIG Supermarket in neighboring town.

PART SEVEN: The Arrival and Early Days

Part Seven includes issues and suggestions that will help you, your family, and your au pair adjust to the new living situation. It will take you from just before arrival, through those exciting but sometimes confusing first few weeks. Part Seven concludes with sections on four important elements of the Au Pair Solution: communication, cooking, "Seasons of the Au Pair Year," and vacation time.

Just Prior to Arrival Day

Everyone in the family will have to adjust to having a new person in your home. The biggest adjustment will likely be for the children. Again, depending on the age of the children, begin to talk with them more specifically about the new au pair's arrival as this date approaches.

Get the children involved in simple preparations — tidying up the au pair's bedroom, making a sign of greeting for the au pair's bedroom door, getting a small plant for her dresser as a "welcome" gesture, coloring picture of things they would like to do with the au pair when she arrives. As a nice touch, place a plant, flower, or chocolate on the au pair's pillow before she arrives.

Remember that your gestures send a message to your au pair — the more you try, the more you expect the au pair to try.

Arrival Day

Depending on the organization you are with, the au pair may travel directly to you or, as with many programs, may fly first to an orientation program of three or four days and then to your home.

The orientation program is a worthwhile means for the au pair to get used to some of the ways of the U.S. while in the company of peers in similar circumstances. The programs I have known have had our new au pair arrive in New York City and join a group of 20 to 40 other new au pairs from various countries. There they room with one or two of them at a hotel where they also have planned orientation classes. The three or four days are then filled with a combination of orientation classes, first aid, CPR, and some touring of the city.

If there is not an orientation program at the beginning of the year's stay, some organizations coordinate a similar regional program which au pairs are required to attend soon after their arrival. These programs are worthwhile and should be supported. They offer a good orientation to the U.S. and an opportunity to meet other au pairs with whom they may want to stay in contact during their year in the U.S.

As mentioned previously, travel arrangements from the arrival city to your home city are your responsibility. Keep in mind when choosing a mode of transportation that the au pair is traveling with one or two heavy suitcases and is anxious to meet you and begin to get to know you.

Fax a Welcome Note

The organizations that conduct orientation programs provide the host families with details of the location, contact numbers, and a general schedule. It is a worthwhile gesture to Fax a note to your arriving au pair at her orientation hotel. Again, it is a confirmation that you are anxiously awaiting her arrival to your family and wishing her well on her arrival. If it is necessary to have the au pair call you during this orientation period, suggest she do so by calling you "collect." Because her orientation/touring schedule is quite full, it is best to have her call you if needed.

First 24 Hours in Your Home

Warmly introduce your new au pair to all family members. Have the children give her a tour of your home, show her to her room, and let her begin to unpack and get settled. Have the au pair call her parents on arrival to let them know she has arrived and is getting acquainted (suggest this first call be at your expense). If you can share a family meal together and then encourage the au pair to continue unpacking and get a good night's rest.

Keep in mind the lingering jet lag your new au pair is likely feeling when she finally arrives at your home. To help her recover more quickly, suggest that she drink plenty of liquids, but no caffeine before bed the first night. It is best to adjust her watch and body clock immediately to the new time zone. Keep encouraging the au pair these first few days to work to adjust to your time zone by staying awake until a reasonable hour at night, getting a good night's sleep, and trying to sleep through to a reasonable morning hour. If she keeps "giving in" to her existing body clock, she will suffer a longer than necessary adjustment to the new time zone.

> ***"When a new au pair arrives, it takes a bit of time for everyone to get used to the change. It's also an exciting opportunity to learn." — Host Parent***

Au Pair's Room — As Her "Sanctuary"

Encourage your au pair immediately to "make herself at home." Within your home, respect your au pair's bedroom as her private sanctuary. This space deserves respect as your au pair's space — everyone should feel obliged to knock before entering and the children should understand they should not freely go in the room when the au pair is not there.

This respect for the au pair's privacy should not absolve them from keeping their room tidy. If you feel a cleaning or tidying up is in order, note that task as part of the week's schedule (see page 89, weekly schedule).

Again, you want to set expectations for "the more you try, the more we try."

The Family That Eats Together

Our family regularly shares dinner at night together often during the week. We have found that it is important to be sure the au pair is often part of that supper hour together. This seems like a simple thing. However, you will find, as the au pair meets a few people and establishes more outside interests, unless you work to have certain set dinnertimes together, you will feel like the changing of shifts — you will arrive home from your day and the au pair will be off to "do their thing" with a "Hello, I'm off" exchanged at the door. The independence is a good thing, just keep a healthy measure of connectedness as well.

"AuPairs often come with a sense of responsibility and stay close to home for the first few months. In almost every case, they develop "wings" after a few months and begin to make new friends. Over time, they become more interested in pursuing their own social life and less interested in the family. Toward the end, it is like hanging onto the reins with both hands." — Host Parent

Try to establish early in the week, what night you will all dine together as an "extended family" and keep that commitment to each other as best you can. Pose some thought provoking questions to the au pair early on that you ask periodically throughout the year — as a "temperature check" of sorts on changing impressions — e. g., What three things do you like the most about living in this country? What three things do you like the least?

First 72 Hours: Time to Observe and Assist

Stay close to home in the early days to observe and assist as your new au pair is getting acquainted with your family, the children, your home, and the overall routine. The best way to be sure this experience gets off to a good start is to be relatively close at hand for these first few days.

> IMPORTANT: *For optimum long-term results, schedule yourself very lightly for the first few days after your au pair's arrival, and not too heavily for the first week or so.*

Take things a bit slowly these first few days but do get on with establishing a sense of normalcy and getting the au pair involved and engaged immediately. Generally we find that "a happy au pair is a busy au pair." Introducing the Standard Operating Procedure manual (below) provides a good framework for "getting into the swing of things" in an organized manner.

Introducing the SOP and Weekly Schedule

Within the first few days of your au pair's arrival you should set aside time to go through your version of the SOP manual. You have already read about this in Part Five and will see in the appendices an example of the one our family uses. I hope that you have already begun to use the enclosed CD-ROM to build and edit your personalized version.

Once again, since English, and certainly "American English," is likely not the au pair's first language, it is extremely helpful to have in writing, through this SOP, many of the details and nuances of your family and the expectations that you want to emphasize and discuss.

Within the first 24 to 72 hours after your au pair's arrival, take time one on one, perhaps over a cup of tea, to go over your SOP page by page. Explain things in more detail as you go through it and be sure the au pair feels free to ask questions. You probably will not want to do this in just one sitting, but do go over all of it within the first few days. This document is a good reference document for you and the au pair if issues become unclear or if you feel you need to reemphasize something you had talked about early on.

This is also a good time to go through the "Weekly Schedule," so that the au pair can get a feel for an average week in your family's life even before the week starts. You may also wish to mention a few of the most important or useful forms from Part Six, such as the "Emergency Phone List" and the "Repeated Event" form.

"It is best to have a written list of responsibilities from day one. They should be reviewed and agreed upon. Later on in the relationship, if the AuPair disagrees about responsibilities, one can refer to the list." — Host Parent

Important: The SOP is a Lot of Material!

Remember to emphasize the SOP covers a lot of material, and that you do not expect her to memorize it! The reason you have an SOP is so that she can look it over at her leisure, and look things up in it if she is not sure what to do.

Driving Lessons

One of the first things you will want to do if the au pair will be expected to drive is to spend a reasonable amount of time these first few days driving together. You will need to familiarize her with your automobile and get comfortable with her skill level. Keep driving together until you are confident that her skill level is such that you trust her driving your car on her own and with your children.

Many of the au pairs we have had living with us had never driven a car with automatic transmission before coming to the U.S. and, in most cases, had never driven an automobile as big as the typical American "family" vehicle. Naturally, the automatic transmission ends up being quite an easy transition for them, but the size of the car (especially a van, station wagon, or sports utility vehicle) does take some getting used to.

Remember as well, that au pairs from the U.K. or Australia/New Zealand have the additional adjustment of driving on the opposite side of the road *and* having the steering wheel on the opposite side of the car. These adjustments will take a bit more time driving together.

Go to a large empty parking lot nearby, and have the au pair sit in the driver's seat. Start with the basics, as you would teaching someone to drive. When you and the au pair are comfortable in the parking lot, go onto the open road and begin to show the her a few of the "landmark" places you will need her to know (schools, friends' houses, etc.), while giving her more time and experience behind the wheel of the family vehicle. Keep in mind the importance of having the au pair in the driver's seat getting to these key places rather than having her be a passenger. Everything about these new surroundings is unique and you need the au pair to connect with landmarks, as a driver, not as an observer taking in the sights. (See also "Driving Policy," in the SOP section.)

In The First Few Weeks

Here are some of the issues that you will want to introduce and deal with after the most crucial ones have been covered in the first few days. Once again, "getting off on the right foot" is important to long-term success. What your au pair becomes used to in the first few days and weeks is what she will expect for the rest of the year.

Weekly Review

Early on, it is useful to spend a few minutes, one on one, talking over the week as it is ending. What things are going well? What things need more focus and improvement? Ask the au pair for her impressions first, then lend your comments to the discussion.

The first few weekly reviews are the most important ones you will have. They may well set the tone for your relationship in the future. Here are a few tips on those all-important first reviews:

- Make sure that you are not tired or stressed when you do meet. Leave plenty of time, especially at first.

- Try to establish a casual and open feeling of rapport.

- Start out with at least a couple of positive comments, things that the au pair has done that you've noticed, appreciated, and wish to encourage.

- If something has occurred during the first week that is a real problem, now is not the time to bring it up. (See Golden Rule #2: Deal with things as they arise. Communicate!)

- Speak slowly, clearly, and directly. Say "You must be in by 10 o'clock on weekday nights" rather than "Perhaps you could attempt to be more conscientious about hitting the hay earlier during the week." If you say the latter, she won't know WHAT you're talking about! Avoid colloquialisms, slang, and very complicated sentence structure. The more important the issue, the more clearly and simply you need to state it!

- Initiate these discussions at the end of the week when you are giving the au pair her pocket money (unless that's a tired or stressful time).

- Give your honest impression of issues that get raised and talk over how you think these things can be worked on and improved. Follow up your discussion `about these items as you both address them in the coming days so you both feel progress is being made toward improvement.

- As discussed in the following checklist, allow the au pair time to explain her point of view when addressing issues.

- Be respectful in tone, especially when discussing problem issues.

- Review the weekly schedule sheet (see page 89) to help you stay focused during these discussions.

A Checklist for the First Few Weeks

Consider using this checklist during the first few weeks to generate discussion on important points:

1._____ Relationship with the children

2._____ Getting necessary tasks done

3._____ Keep good record of house account $$ money

4._____ Driving

5._____ Progress on deciding what educational class to take

6._____ Things that are going well

7._____ Things that need more attention/improvement

Again, start by asking for the au pair's input on these points, to get the conversation going. Add your comments and observations to broaden the discussion. As your time together increases, if all is going well, you will feel less of a need for regular weekly discussions. Offer it anyway, in case the au pair would like to bring some things up that you may be unaware of. If all is well, then reinforce this fact and carry on.

Developing Friendships and Interests

Within the first few weeks you will want to be encouraging your au pair to work at developing friendships and finding courses and outside activities of interest. It is important that the au pair be getting used to your family and your children and also be starting to establish relationships and class activities outside of your home to expand their experience further. The local coordinator will be helpful with this, through their personal visit once the au pair arrives and through cluster meetings.

It is important that you also be involved and conscious of the external connectedness needed to make the au pair's experience broader and more worthwhile. Probe somewhat with your au pair to establish areas of interest and then "brainstorm" some ideas on how to pursue these interests locally. We have had au pairs "audit" courses at local schools; volunteer in pre-school classrooms and at the local hospital. All of these things are worthwhile and get the au pair out in broader circles, experiencing different aspects of your local community and culture first hand.

As you would with a teenage child, ask to meet and be introduced to friends your au pair is spending time with. Remember, you are the au pair's host parents for this period of time and overseeing the company your au pair is keeping is an aspect of this. If you feel it is important to comment about the company your au pair is keeping, do so tactfully and with sensitivity. As a young adult, possibly living away from home for the first extended period of time, the au pair is establishing their independence and may resist somewhat your comments. Give guidance and feedback as you feel it is appropriate and in the best interests of your au pair and your developing relationship with your au pair.

When Friends Visit Your Au Pair

It should be understood with your au pair that she will still have responsibilities in your family even when a friend or family member is visiting (unless of course the au pair is on vacation also). It even is sometimes important to point this out when local friends/au pairs are visiting during an evening of babysitting. You do not want your child/children to feel ignored nor excluded because a few au pairs are visiting and, though in the same room together, are speaking their native language. Simply observed and simply stated by you calls the issue to the au pairs attention and tends to solve it.

Phone and Long Distance Communication Issues

Some au pairs are more prone to long distance phone calls, and their related expense, than others. Unlike Europe, phone bills in the U.S. are relatively easy to decipher in allocating individual call expenses, so having the au pair determine their expense for the month is easy. It may, in some cases, especially early on, be a shock when they see how much their casual calls to family and friends at home cost them for the month.

Early on, show the au pair how your phone bill is set up, with each individual call noted, so they know what to expect. When the monthly bill arrives, have the au pair review it, noting their calls and adding them up to determine what they owe you.

If the au pair seems to be having a particularly hard time disciplining themselves relative to phone expenses, you might consider having them get themselves pre-paid phone cards. That way they can decide upfront what money they can afford to spend on phone calls. When the phone card is used up, so are their allocated funds.

Faxes are a quick means of communicating with family at home. If the au pair has access to a fax machine, as they do in our house, this can be a convenient way to correspond with family. Here too, the call expense can be noted from the monthly phone bills.

Email and Internet access have become a more commonplace tool within many families, including ours. Depending on your service provider and your monthly rate plan — determine what, if any, limitations you feel the need to set relative to connect time. In our home, I ask that the au pair monitor and reimburse me for connect time longer than 5 minutes at one sitting. I also ask the au pair to "connect" when the family, kids are not at home so the computer is free for general family use and homework when needed.

Communication in General

The au pair is a new occupant in your household and family. Communicate with her as you would any member of the family. This includes the most normal and regular greetings (e.g., "Good morning" "See you, I'm leaving now, have a good day. What are your big plans today?" "Hi, I'm home!" "How was your day?" "Anything new with the children?" "Hi, how was the movie?" "Goodnight, I'm going to bed") as well as the more directed discussions about the plans for the day.

Feeling "At Home"

One of the ways to help your au pair feel at home in your family is to include her in the regular banter that goes on around the house. You should initiate these greetings yourself, thus encouraging your au pair to reciprocate. There is nothing more awkward than having an additional person living with you who, by your actions or hers, is made to feel and acts "invisible" (e.g., the au pair comes in from being out for the evening, walks by you in an open room watching TV and heads directly to her bedroom without your saying a word to each other.

Often a simple hello is all that is needed. This is not a stranger rooming in your home. The au pair needs to be and feel a part of your family. You can help her in small ways, such as saving articles about the country she hails from that you come across in daily newspapers, or other publications.

In Person, and Not

While most communication is best done in person, do establish as well the common courtesy of leaving notes for each other if you are going out and cannot speak in person. In our family, the weekly schedule is always on the kitchen counter and that is also the place to look for phone messages taken or a note about each other's whereabouts. We have a kitchen drawer full of scrap paper on which to write notes, phone messages, grocery lists, etc.

Who's the Contact Person?

Determine in your family who the main contact/supervisor is for the au pair. In our family, I am our au pair's primary contact person. This relationship is very important to establish right from the start so the au pair is clear about who is her key point of contact and clarification.

This does not mean my husband cannot "sub" for me and clarify a situation that arises in my absence. But it does mean that I am the first person the au pair looks to for guidance, and that our relationship is primary. My husband occasionally adds particular emphasis to a point or issue that needs to be reiterated (e.g., safe driving). Having both of us speak to a particular issue adds weight to the importance of the issue and illustrates our united concern.

> *"In our family, as wife and mother, I am the primary adult contact with our au pair. My husband reads the applications and we agree on priorities, but I am the person who carries this out with the au pair. My sense has been that he intimidates the au pairs and it is best if I handle most aspects of the relationship." — Host Parent*

In terms of communication with the au pair and her responsibilities, your best practice, as with the best supervisor/subordinate relationships, is to keep the communication regular and "as it happens." Explain what it is you need done and how you want it done. If you feel clarification is needed to fine tune, give that feedback immediately for the best results. Always use the common courtesy of giving constructive comments/feedback in a way that is most comfortable and effective for the au pair, generally when you are alone together.

What the Children Say

Children of grammar school age and older can provide temperature checks as well on how things are going with your au pair. Pay attention to this and evaluate it for what it is.

Early on with a new au pair, I have often found that minor frustrations the children are experiencing are in fact situations in which they need to communicate more effectively their own needs in a pleasant way. You can help by having their food/snack preferences and schedules written down, but there will also be times when the children need to be more patient with the au pair's growing familiarity with them and learning to communicate more directly their wishes and needs.

Having the children establish a stronger sense of their own needs and be able to express these tactfully to the au pair is a maturation opportunity for them also. Naturally, if the children are raising particular areas of concern (e.g., a "close call" driving the car), do discuss it with the au pair.

Visiting friends and family can also provide important observations about how the au pair is doing. Listen to their comments. They know your family, your children, and your values, and their comments can be helpful to you as objective input. Here too, follow up with discussions with the au pair on any issues you find troubling.

Early Adjustment in General

Although integration will take a little while, first impressions will be important. Although unlikely, be aware of early signs of homesickness or other difficulties adjusting.

Ask your children for their impressions. Watch for signals from them as their relationship with the au pair is developing. Address any areas of concern immediately and directly and, if appropriate, discuss these things with your au pair.

Also use your local coordinator as a sounding board if you have any serious concerns that you are having difficulty resolving within the family.

The Golden Rules

Once again, a few simple rules can have a tremendous impact on your au pair relationship. I'll add a third one now, a rule that applies more to the host family parent(s) than to the au pair herself (especially those, like us, who are "repeat customers.". These rules cannot be repeated, or considered, too often:

Everyone should try as hard as possible to make this work well.

Deal immediately with things that arise. Don't let aggravation fester.

And the new rule, if you become a "repeat customer" of the Au Pair Solution:

Work constantly at keeping your current situation "fresh." While this may be a repeat year for you with a new au pair, keep in mind that it is your current au pair's first and only experience. Make it worthwhile.

"The most difficult situation I've had is when our au pair stayed out quite late the night before my husband and I were to take a trip. I woke up at midnight and couldn't get back to sleep, worrying about her and wondering when she'd get home.

When I heard her come in, I told her that I was up worried about her and in order for me to go away, I needed peace of mind about my help being there for the kids. I did not scold her because I never told her when I expected her in that night, so we made a rule and now she knows. She was totally fine about the way the situation was handled and she apologized to me and said it would never happen again. When I left in the a.m. she had left a very kind note on my luggage.

Communication is very important. They need to know "where you're coming from" so they understand the importance of what it is you request them to do." — Host Parent

Meals and Cooking

It is my experience that cooking, in a new country, takes time for the au pair to get used to. Although some things look somewhat familiar, everything has a different name, and the meat cuts and fish look quite different. Keep this in mind for your au pair and have 15 to 25 specific main dishes/recipes in mind that your children like. I am a big advocate of "gourmet on the go" and combine easy, tasty recipes collected over the years with easy quasi-European dishes that are often family recipes. The recipes in my various cookbooks are always marked off with a commentary in pencil as to how people liked it, what it needed more or less of, etc. If it was a "loser" at the family dinner table, we don't bother with it again.

The Recipe Lists (page 102) help to present your au pair with a variety of options for dinner planning. This list is on the CD-ROM, so that you can easily customize it, and enlarge it as your au pair gains confidence in her "American" cooking skills.

Try a Kids' Cookbook, and Take Time to Help at First

There are many kids' cookbooks, in which the language, instructions, and ingredients are quite simple. Consider starting with a few recipes from a kids' cookbook or a very basic cookbook that couples often get as wedding gifts as they are setting up a household and getting used to cooking more balanced and healthier meals.

Take time in the first few weeks to make these dishes at least once with the au pair (again, as with driving, have the au pair do the preparation with your encouragement and counsel) so she has a "visual" recollection of how the dish is made and how it looks when done. Lasagna may be a staple in your house, but an au pair from Poland may have never seen even a picture of it to associate with. When you have cycled through your list of meals together, have the au pair then keep rotating through this preferred list so the children get a good variety of food they are used to and like.

"E-Z" Cookery?

As you know, there are many easy-to-cook items available in the grocery store. I encourage the au pair to stick with my preferred list of meals and only try those "just add meat" quick items on rare occasions when time doesn't allow for anything more. We don't allow TV dinners or microwave dinners as a substitute for a fresh cooked meal, although in some families these may be acceptable. Give immediate feedback about meals so your au pair can keep honing this skill and keep improving the reception from your family.

Please also see page 102 in Part Six for some guides on helping your au pair know what to cook and when. These will help her to serve the meals that your family enjoys.

Shopping Made Easy

When writing your grocery list be very specific about ingredients needed, and even generally where things can be found in the supermarket (e.g., with spices; with baking items). If you prefer specific brand name items, specify that on your grocery list. The "Where to Get What" Shopping Chart (page 103, and on CD-ROM) will help your au pair to shop most efficiently.

As the au pair gets more comfortable cooking, encourage her to try some new recipes she may come across and think your family will enjoy, or to share a recipe from her home country (especially a holiday traditional dish). I always tell our au pairs, that this is a wonderful opportunity for them to be creative in the kitchen at our expense.

Seasons of the Au Pair Year

Each year has its seasons and so, it seems, does the tempo of the year with an au pair. It's well worth a moment of thought about what I call the "biorhythms" of the year.

In the Beginning

There is a bit of euphoria about many first time experiences in a totally new environment with new people. Au pairs are very often living for the first extended time away from their families and are certainly feeling a new found sense of freedom and discovery.

The "Honeymoon" Ends

After a few weeks, when life settles into more of a routine, your au pair may start to think "is this all there is?" and that "this is basically work." The "honeymoon" period is over, and the patterns of the days and weeks tend to get more familiar and a bit mundane. This is normal. You should not get discouraged by this, and you certainly should not take this personally. Help moderate the cycles by encouraging the au pair to develop peer relationships outside of your family, identify outside interests and coursework to pursue, make arrangements for a fun outing together that everyone can look forward to (e.g., a cultural outing in town, a car trip together over the weekend to another city). This can help maintain a healthy sense of discovery and excitement about your au pair's year away. Moderate mood swings are quite normal. Do not take them personally and simply do your best to keep them moderate.

Au Pair Educational Component

An important requirement which the au pair must satisfy during the year exchange relates to her taking the equivalent of six academic credit hours of coursework. As the host family, you are obligated to provide up to a maximum of $500 over the course of a year toward an au pair's educational pursuits.

The USIA has given the organizations certain guidelines as to what type of coursework satisfies this requirement and your local coordinator can help guide you and your au pair in making proper choices, mindful of the au pair's interests, course availability, and cost. Not satisfying this requirement can put an au pair in violation of visa terms and compromise receiving her completion certificate and security deposit at year end. Encourage your au pair to get started with fulfilling her educational responsibilities within the first month or two of arrival. Attending classes is another means of getting the au pair out experiencing a new culture, meeting new people.

Recognize how intimidating it can be for your au pair dealing with the bureaucracy of an educational institution, knowing the right questions to ask, being able to express oneself in another language. Help where you can by collecting brochures, newspaper ads, program literature to share with your au pair. Offer to make some targeted phone call inquiries and offer support and advice in making a decision about which courses to pursue. Support your au pair in her consideration of academic or career related classes that will be helpful in future career endeavors.

In addition to taking classes, host parents should suggest other ways in which the au pair's future interests could be further clarified through experiences such as doing volunteer work, attending seminars and lectures in subjects of interest. In addition to taking classes, we have had au pairs volunteer at our childrens' school, serve as a hospital aide a few hours per week, help in the exercising, care and feeding of horses at a local stable, and coach a local girls basketball team. All of these experiences were tremendously satisfying to the individual au pairs and strengthened their self-confidence.

Birthdays and Holidays

Even after settling in to a comfortable routine, your au pair will still have highs and lows: holiday times; news of a friend or cousin getting married and the realization that she will miss the event; a death in her extended family; her birthday; a local au pair friend's year coming to an end as she heads off for her 13th month of travel and then home, leaving your au pair behind. All of these "pulls" to home ought to balance somewhat with the new experiences in her host environment. Keep the year in focus for the au pair. Help her feel included in family happenings and events that will add to her memories, experiences and ultimately her personal growth.

In Europe, birthdays are much more cause for family celebration than in the U.S. The birthday person often "holds court" at home all day, greeting family and friends who are expected to stop by to extend their good wishes (congratulating both the birthday celebrant and the parents) and have some cake and tea or coffee. Understanding this, make the effort to celebrate your au pair's birthday in a fun way as a family and encourage her to include her local friends in sharing the birthday cake, going out together afterward, etc.

Quarterly Reviews

Some of the au pair organizations have established written quarterly or six-month reviews. These can be beneficial and are an additional opportunity for communication. As with performance reviews in a work environment, if you have established good ongoing communication, there should be no surprises in these more formal periodic reviews. If your au pair organization requires periodic written reviews, the local coordinator may be in contact with you requesting a copy of the review and seeking a brief phone discussion with you on the points made.

Vacation Time

Knowing how to handle vacations and holidays with and without your au pair's participation is an important way to avoid additional tension during stressful times.

Your Au Pair's Vacation

Although it might seem premature, it is in your best interest to decide as early as possible when you want the au pair to take her two weeks of paid vacation. Inform her as soon as you know so she can start thinking about it and making plans for those weeks. If you know it even before she leaves her home country, mention it to her. She may have a family member or a friend who is considering taking advantage of her being in the U.S. to come for a visit. Your au pair's time off may be a perfect time for this "reunion," when there is a companion available to travel with.

The time you identify as vacation time for the au pair may be time you need to be away on your own as a nuclear family. Be sure these plans are set up well in advance so that your au pair can feel secure in making plans and arrangements ahead of time.

If the au pair is staying home during your absence, encourage her to plan day trips or a long weekend trip to a nice place a reasonable distance from you. It is important to encourage the au pair to have a change of scenery for some portion of her vacation time. Usually, vacationing on her own is an event that the au pair is excited about and can look forward to. Again, even if you live in a lovely place where other people come to vacation, you should encourage the au pair to "get away" during her vacation time. It is important for her to feel a distinct sense of time away from the family and her normal responsibilities so she will likewise feel refreshed and renewed at the end of it.

Following is a list of travel services that have a reasonably priced product targeted to the au pair/student exchange market, offering worthwhile trips throughout the country for weekend get-aways, 9 days to 2 weeks during the entire year:

AMERICAN ADVENTURE
105 Hancock Street   Tel.: 1-800-873-5872   1-800-TREK-USA
Quincy, MA 02169-2114   Fax: 1-617-984-2045   amadusa@attmail.com

CULTURAL HIGHWAYS
P.O. Box 4191   Tel.: 1-203-949-0396   1-800-819-7683
Wallingford, CT 06492   Fax: 1-203-284-0815   chiways@aol.com
                              www.cultural_hi_ways.com

HOSTELING INTERNATIONAL
733 15th Street - Suite #840   Tel: 1-800-444-6111
Washington, DC 20005   Web: www.hiayh.org

GREEN TORTOISE ADVENTURE TRAVEL
494 Broadway   Tel.: 1-415-956-7500   1-800-867-8647
San Francisco, CA 94133   info@greentortoise.com

TREK AMERICA
P.O. Box 189   Tel.: 1-800-221-0596
Rockaway, NJ 07866   info@trekamerican.com   www.trek.america.com

AMERICAN ADVENTURES
9741 Canoga Ave.   Tel.: 1-818-721-6000   1-800-873-5872
Chatsworth, CA 91311   Fax: 1-818-993-7941   amadlax@att.net
                               www.americanadventures.com

Vacationing With Your Au Pair

If your children are young, you may want to take the au pair with you on your family vacation. In this case, you will need to identify two other weeks that will work for the au pair to be away , during which time you will have to arrange for alternative childcare.

When the au pair will be vacationing with you to help with the children, again, mention the plans early on and clearly present it as the "perk" that it is being in fun and different surroundings. Your au pair will appreciate the opportunity to experience new places at no cost to her. As you would at home, set schedules and expectations for your au pair during vacations.   Be clear with her of on-and off-duty time so there is good understanding of your needs in these new surroundings.

Vacationing Without Your Au Pair

When planning trips that do not include your au pair, be clear what you expect of her during your absence. Again, give the au pair as much advance notice as possible. Issues to consider may include the following:

- Will the au pair be free to stay alone at your home on her own ?

- Can a local friend be invited to spend the night while you are away?

- Will the au pair have responsibilities/things to take care of in your absence ?

- Do you need a ride to and from the airport/train station ?

- What are the rules in terms of car use while you are away?

- Will any of these days be considered paid vacation days? If so, is the au pair free to plan a trip during this time period?

As you would when you are away for an evening, be sure to tell the au pair where you are and how to contact you in an emergency. Sometimes we loan the au pair the cellular phone for easier communication. Be sensitive and minimize holidays when the au pair is on her own. If she were at home, she would likely be spending time with her own family. It can be a lonely time, so keep it to a minimum.

Holidays

To the extent it is possible and practical, take the au pair with you as part of your family during big holidays (e.g. Christmas/Hanukkah, Thanksgiving, 4th of July) Keep in mind that the au pair is far from home and is relying on you as "family" during this year. Make her a part of your holiday celebrations whenever possible. Take the time beforehand to tell her what to expect, who will be there, what she should wear, what responsibilities she will have while there, etc. In our family, I always ask the au pair to "pitch right in" and help wherever and however she can. When an au pair is considered part of the family and not a guest, she is more likely to contribute appropriately.

And Lastly, Your Au Pair's Family's Vacations

If family member(s) or friends from the au pair's home country have expressed interest in coming to visit, you must decide, as a family, what your limitations are in terms of hosting them in your home. You may or may not be prepared to have them stay in your home for a short period of time while visiting your au pair.

We have found that one week for one family member/or one friend is our limit and even at that, we ask that the visitor be "housed" in our au pair's room with our au pair. (This works for most circumstances except "boyfriends" of a female au pair, where we have still been willing to have him stay in our home but have made accommodation for him elsewhere in the house and for less than 1 week.) There are nice and reasonably priced "bed and breakfast" places in a neighboring town to us and I offer those contact numbers as an option to consider.

PART EIGHT: Trouble Shooting for Common Problems

It is difficult to generalize the nature of the early difficulties you may have with a new person joining your household. Besides early homesickness, and fatigue adjusting to the new time zone, the most common problems usually revolve around misunderstandings about the au pair's responsibilities. As your au pair comes in more contact with other au pairs, issues may arise regarding what other au pairs do versus what you ask your au pair to do. I tend to rely on the Standard Operating Procedures manual as my best means of drawing us both back to established expectations.

In the following sections I address a few common problems, some clearly more serious than others.

Time Keepers

You will find that some au pair's are avid "time keepers," keeping track of every minute that they are "on duty" and feeling they must totally disassociate themselves from the children when "off duty." This can be an issue with small children who do not necessarily understand "leaving the au pair alone." Explain to the au pair that you are all living in the same home space and, unless she locks her bedroom door or physically leaves the house, she is in the family and needs to be flexible and understanding, especially with small children. In our family, I have always kept in mind that the unusual heavy week generally gets balanced out with much lighter weeks. The key is to be flexible and look at the overall schedule as opposed to the burden of a single day or an unusually busy week.

Car Problems (Constantly Lost, Accidents, etc.)

Much of getting oriented will require your au pair to spend time with an area map showing where you are and where/in which direction her destinations are, as well as clearly written directions on how to get from "here to there." Our map file of typed directions gets much use in the early months with a new au pair. Have the au pair describe to you the way she was intending to go and clarify with her the most direct route. Encourage the au pair to always ask questions when she is unsure of the way. Most people will be extremely helpful when asked for directions.

The strain of car accidents is something I wish every host family could avoid. Just remember, you too were an inexperienced driver once. Spend adequate time early on driving with the au pair to help her get used to your automobile, and to get comfortable with her driving ability. When you go places together, sometimes have the au pair drive so you can monitor her driving and give immediate feedback. Ask for feedback from other responsible adults (e.g. grandparents) who may occasionally ride with the au pair.

On a particularly rainy or snowy night do not be hesitant to tell the au pair that she may not use the car to go out. Remember, you would restrict your own young adult from driving in bad weather. Do not take chances with the au pair.

If the au pair does have the misfortune of having a car accident during her year with you, as part of the learning experience and feedback, be sure to have her take responsibility for filing the necessary accident reports, make clarifying phone calls, feeling the inconvenience of having a car in the shop being fixed, paying you back for the requisite insurance deductible, etc.

As uncomfortable as this is for the au pair, it is part of the "lesson learned" and is what you want her to remember when she is again driving. We have gone so far as to restrict the use of the car radio for an au pair who seemed accident prone well into her year with us. You may want to significantly restrict your au pair's personal use of the car for a month following an accident. Use common sense in choosing such consequences.

Overly Argumentative Personality

This type of personality can be exasperating in your own child, and is as well in an au pair. Sometimes the style is cultural, sometimes just characteristic of the individual. In any case, it is best to gently call attention to it by citing specific examples so your message is clear. Encourage the au pair to examine this pattern of behavior in herself, explaining that it is a negative quality that is putting unnecessary strain on everyone. Explain that she needs to be mindful of it and work to change her behavior.

Questionable Friends

As you would give feedback and influence your children about the people they associate with, so too you may find it necessary to intervene and comment about to the individual(s) the au pair is spending time with. Again, give tactful feedback. Ask questions, give your opinions. As host parents, you are the surrogate parents of this au pair for the year. Be clear on what your opinions are and what you consider "right" and "wrong" relative to friendships, casual associations, and appropriate places/things to see and do.

Keep in mind that you are dealing with a young adult who is living away from home, possibly for the first time, and trying to establish her independence. Accordingly, your opinions about friends/associates may not be listened to as seriously as you would like. This is normal, but should not preclude you from expressing your opinions and concerns tactfully.

"Party Animals"

Be very clear about your expectations and curfews on weekdays and weeknights. You will read in the example Standard Operating Procedures manual how I have addressed this for our household. I am always clear about where we are going and how to reach us in an emergency. I expect a similar courtesy in knowing where the au pair is going, the company she will be in, generally what time she expects to be home, etc.

It is important to be very clear about the seriousness of drinking and driving with both the au pair and anyone with whom she may associate. I am always clear about the fact that I will come and pick her up from any situation she may find herself in, in which she or the person she came with is not fit to drive safely. The au pair must know that drinking and driving or any involvement with drugs would be considered grounds for immediate dismissal.

You may take comfort in knowing that as a result of a much healthier upbringing and attitude about alcohol consumption, young Europeans rarely engage in binge drinking the way young Americans do.

Who Owns the Problem?

Quite a few problems that develop have little to do with the au pair and relate instead simply to having an additional person in your household. Keep this in mind as you make adjustments sharing your household with another person (e.g., different sleeping habits, somewhat different eating preferences, etc.).

In many problem situations, the au pair may be the "designated problem person," but the problem may actually be caused by the "fit" between the au pair and your family. You, as the host parent and primary contact person, must "own" (take responsibility for) any problems that develop from the start. For example, remembering that your husband is a very private person may help you to determine if the au pair's use of the family TV is out of line, or if you would be better served by obtaining an inexpensive extra TV for the au pair's room to provide your husband with the privacy he needs.

Keeping Problems in Perspective

It is best not to make too much of minor disagreements. Communicate, talk them through, review your expectations, highlight the many positives and the fact that every family's circumstances and needs are different. End by explaining what you are asking for is quite reasonable, given the guidelines and the general ebb and flow of the schedule.

Keep a proper perspective on issues that come up. If the au pair is doing a very commendable job getting to know your children and handling her duties, the fact that she tends to sleep in until noon on days off, should not be of serious concern to you.

It can't be emphasized too strongly:

Everybody should try as hard as possible to make this work well!

Bringing in the Local Coordinator

Do not rely on a third party (the local coordinator) for communications that should have begun within your own household, between you and the au pair. If you or the au pair use outsiders (the local coordinator) to deal with issues fundamental to your household, it becomes increasingly difficult to establish good and ongoing communication within the household, and the level of trust in each other will deteriorate. If you cannot resolve the issue through good communication and discussion, you should make the local coordinator aware of the problem. Be clear with the coordinator about the circumstances and the steps you have taken so far. Ask the coordinator for advice and support in resolving it.

When It Can't Be Fixed

In our approximately two decades of having au pairs, there have been varying circumstances that have been cause for changing the au pair. These have ranged from "homesickness" to "this isn't at all what I thought it was going to be like" to "I have decided I do want to be in a family with younger children/fewer children" to the most extreme "my boyfriend now says he wants to marry me but I must come home as soon as possible."

In the course of having a number of successive au pairs, you will likely experience an unsuccessful match. Call your local coordinator at the first sign of difficulty *that you cannot resolve within your household.* The coordinator can advise you, can help intervene with the au pair as a more objective third party, and can declare an end to trying to fix an unresolvable situation.

We have had au pairs that we have liked more than others, but I have not yet been successful at "fixing" a serious problem despite my 20-plus years as a human resources executive. In three out of four changeouts, the au pairs left my home and returned to their home country. One au pair left our family and was rematched with another family with much younger children.

The au pair organizations wear a few hats when a match turns out to be unsuccessful. They have an obligation to you, the host family, to deliver a successful match, and they have an obligation to their foreign exchange au pair to attempt to deliver a successful one-year program experience. This is your family, your children — be clear when a match is not working and state what it is that you need to fix it. If you need this au pair to leave your family and you want another au pair state that objective clearly to the organization. Find out what the time frame will be for getting another au pair. Do you want the current au pair to remain with your family in this interim, or will you make other childcare arrangements until a replacement arrives?

Each organization has specific policies about replacing an au pair and helping with a rematch. Read through these policies carefully in the materials you are given. Understand these terms relative to both the organization's obligations to you in successfully placing an au pair and the financial implications of a rematch. In my experience, an organization that is committed to the host family, will work diligently on finding a successful rematch with no additional financial burden on the family. Some even offer pro-rated "relief" to the host family if there is a short period of time without an au pair in place. The organizations have their reputations to uphold with existing and prospective families. If you are and will likely continue to be a suitable host family for their program, they will work diligently to maintain your loyalty and satisfaction.

In-Country Rematches versus Starting Over

In the event of a rematch, the organization may propose two possibilities. (1) They may have an au pair "in-country" already who is herself looking for a rematch from her current host family, or (2) You may start the sourcing, and matching, and interviewing process again, targeting the earliest possible arrival date.

There may indeed be an au pair match that works "on the rebound" for your family that did not in an initial placement. Our family has chosen to start over again. The timing can be quite different between these two alternatives. An in-country rematch may be accomplished in a matter of days as opposed to weeks to start the placement process over again from the beginning.

Read the language of your organization's agreement on these issues to understand how your paid-in fees will be credited in the case of a rematch. Our experience has been that the organization ensures you are "credited" for time without an au pair and does not require you to pay additional funds to complete a rematch.

Those Golden Rules Again

They can't be said too often:

Everyone should try as hard as possible to make this work well.

Deal immediately with things that arise. Don't let aggravation fester.

And, for "repeat customers":

Work constantly at keeping your current situation "fresh." While this may be a repeat year for you with a new au pair, it is your current au pair's first and only experience. Make it worthwhile.

PART NINE: Saying Goodbye

After you reach the six-month point of the au pair's stay, the months together seem to fly by. By the ninth month, the au pair organization will be contacting you to reapply for the following year, and will be having the au pair make arrangements to return home.

Be Ready for Next Year

Get your materials updated and submitted as soon as possible to give yourselves plenty of time to consider the best candidates the organization has to offer you. Discuss departure arrangements with your current au pair so you are clear about departure dates, any overlap with a new au pair, travel plans for the current au pair's 13th month, and any family plans and schedules to consider in light of this transition.

With the various plans you and the au pair are making at this time, the children may get some sense of these discussions. As suggested in earlier sections, with smaller children, keep extended discussions about the au pair's departure to a minimum until about two weeks before her departure, so as not to create any unnecessary anxiety. At this point, if a new au pair is coming, you can combine this discussion with creating some excitement about another au pair arriving.

You might consider involving children 8 to 10 years old and older, as well as your current au pair, in reading the applications of potential au pairs input. Keep in mind however, that the final decision is up to you.

Overlap with a New Au Pair

If your family chooses to continue with this type of childcare, as noted on page 48, you may consider a few days' overlap of the new au pair and your departing au pair. It will depend of course on the circumstances of your year together and the practical timing of the changeover. It can be a big help to have the experienced au pair help initiate the new au pair, but the decision each year about overlap should be made independently.

13th Month Travel Plans

The J-1 student visa which au pairs hold specifies a 13-month period: 12 months with the host family plus a 13th month earmarked for travel on their own before returning to their home country. This 13th month of travel is taken at each au pair's option, as it is unpaid time relative to the program itself. If the au pair has the financial means to travel at the end of her stay, it can be a wonderful concluding adventure before heading home. Your au pair may need your help in making arrangements for her 13th month of travel.

Again, the same travel organizations mentioned on page 118, who cater to au pair and student exchange programs, offer reasonably priced trips to consider during this 13th month. Work with the au pair to clarify departure dates, and trip duration, and to coordinate all of this with her flight home and your new au pair's arrival. You may find there is a day or so when the au pair is "in transit" from her 13th month of travel and her flight home. If it is not disruptive to younger children adjusting to the new au pair, you might offer to have her spend that day or so with your family. You might also offer to hold some of your au pair's baggage while she travels on her 13th month trip.

Au pairs tend to accumulate additional clothing and memorabilia during their year and will likely find their original bag(s) insufficient for their trip home. If your au pair has any family members or friends visiting during the year, have her consider sending a bag home with the returning friend. Air freight to ship things home is prohibitively expensive. Shipping by boat is considerably less expensive but can take six to eight weeks.

Growth Areas for the Au Pair from the Year Abroad

There are undoubtedly areas of development you and the au pair will have noticed over the course of your year together. These are worth highlighting with the au pair as the year is coming to an end. They may include:

- Improved fluency in a foreign language

- Considerable experience and understanding of another culture

- Greater willingness to try new things. More confidence meeting new people, and experiencing new situations

- Broader, more objective understanding of her home country and brethren

- Increased independence and sense of responsibility

- Stronger understanding of herself, her strengths and weaknesses

- Greater acceptance of other people's differences

- Greater ability to face problems and try to resolve them

- Increases ability to reach out and ask for help from others

Documentation to Help Your Au Pair

If your au pair took part in courses or volunteer actvities during the year, encourage her to get letters from the teacher/organization describing her participation. This "certification" of experiences while abroad will be valuable documentation as she seeks entry into the job market at home or continues her education. Europe, especially, values internship experiences and these letters will be useful to facilitate the au pair's "next steps."

"I have a favour to ask of you. If it's not too much trouble, could you please write me a letter of recommendation and mail it to me? There's no rush, but it would be nice to have - and show a future employer. You probably know me better than any employer... it would be really great if you could do that for me! Thanks in advance!" — Au Pair

A Letter of Support

A sample letter for the au pair to take back home (also on CD) that documents some of what she did while here. Use the CD-ROM version to customize this important document for your au pair's benefit.

---

date

TO WHOM IT MAY CONCERN:

It is with great pleasure that I write a personal recommendation on behalf of _____ of (home city, country).

I came to know _____ in the year she spent living with our family (date to date) on an exchange program through (organization name) of (location of organization) when she was ___ years old. She had listed connections she hoped to make within the American communities with which she would have contact, and, while here, went about seizing on opportunities available to her during the course of her stay to follow through. _____ also took advantage of her time here to volunteer three days a week in the kindergarten program of a prestigious northeastern private grammar and middle school, working with children ages five and six years old. She also involved herself in sports classes and activities, and took ceramics classes.

We found _____'s enthusiasm and sense of curiosity about her new-found surroundings refreshing.   While in the U.S., she went on several travel excursions, especially in the northeast and to the Pacific northwest. ____ obviously greatly enjoyed the new experiences and the people with whom she made contact.

We found ___ to be an extremely responsible and trustworthy person: she took significant responsibility in handling many aspects of organizing and running a busy household of __ adults and ___ children. She is mature and self-motivated about everything she undertakes; she is well-mannered and well-bred. Her English was excellent right from the start.

In general, and without reservation, I wholeheartedly recommend _____ for future endeavors she may entertain. I am confident she will be successful in whatever she pursues.

Sincerely,

(host parent)

A Life-Shaping Year

This will have been a life-shaping year for the au pair, and reentry into her home country's culture will likely result in a bit of reverse culture shock. It may be helpful to explain to your au pair that, after a year of considerable growth and new experiences, she will return home expecting friends and family to have had similar life-changing developments. The surprise, in many cases, is that the year has been just a normal passage of time with very few changes. The au pair will need to adjust her expectations accordingly and also moderate somewhat her enthusiasm about her year away. Many friends have never had such a life-framing experience and may not be able to relate to it.

Explain that, while she will gradually adjust to being home, she will always have a special place in her mind and heart for the changes and growth she experienced living abroad. Some of the friendships nurtured in her year away will continue after she returns. These are friends with whom she shared a very special developmental time in her young life, friends who will always understand the experiences in a way that even a best friend cannot.

"How are you doing? I hope everyone is fine. It is such a long time ago that I have heard news from the Liebermann family, and I am really interested. Are the children as active as I remember them?

I am still working with a small company as a foreign-language secretary. I would like to let you know you will always have an open invitation to stay with us when you are in Germany. Please write back and keep in touch." — Au Pair

Saying Good-bye, A Final Party, and Staying in Touch

As the week before your au pair's departure approaches, think about how you want the family to say their good-byes. You may want to plan a nice family dinner together and then invite the au pair's local friends to join you for dessert. We have had our departing au pair arrange a "make your own ice cream sundae" party at our home as a way to say good-bye to all the local friends she made, as well as to introduce the new au pair to these same people.

Be sure to exchange contact numbers, mailing addresses, and Email addresses with your departing au pair to keep in touch. Put the au pair on your holiday letter list so she will get annual family updates. The children especially will appreciate keeping in touch with the au pair after her departure. A letter from a departed au pair is always a cause for joy and continuing interest.

Conclusion

Making This Work for Everyone

My objective in writing this book was to emphasize the significant attributes of this live-in childcare alternative and provide practical "How-To's" to make this arrangement productive and successful for the host family and the visiting au pair. Ultimately, I hope to make the learning curve significantly shorter and steeper for all parties involved to further ensure early success with this arrangement.

As a family, we have gotten to this level of understanding through years of acting from our instincts, combined with lessons of managing people successfully, trial and error and gradually establishing better understandings and guidelines for what works best for us. You will need to rely on your instincts some also. But by using many of the practical suggestions provided here, you can establish a firm sense of what your needs are, the general type of individual you are seeking, and guidelines to successfully manage this important process.

Customize a Standard Operating Procedure (SOP), au pair spec, and weekly schedule for your family via hard copy or using the enclosed CD-ROM, from the templates provided. Your efforts on the front end of this process, defining your needs and those of your family, will ensure a better matching and selection process and a more rewarding experience overall. Keep the spec and SOP evergreen by adding to it as issues come up and revisiting it at year-end. Then think about how your family's needs have changed as you consider hosting a new au pair.

Keep in mind the general "Golden Rules of Thumb" mentioned throughout this book:

Everyone should try as hard as possible to make this work well.

Deal immediately with things that arise. Do not let aggravation fester.

Constantly work at keeping your current situation "fresh." This may be a repeat year for your family, but it is your current au pair's first and perhaps only experience with this remarkable program.

At the end of the day, one small aspect done better for your family, or one small mistake avoided, is worth many times the cost of this book.

Enclosed is a preaddressed postcard on which to write comments or suggestions you might have for additions to this book or to let us know of someone you feel might also benefit from this book (we will send them a brief description and an optional purchase postcard).

Charts and Forms: Hard Copy

I've provided hard copies of various forms and charts here, as you may find it more convenient to photocopy some of them, rather than printing them, customized or not, from the CD-ROM. Those of you who prefer not to use a computer will find these to be of great value. Also, in many cases, it may be more convenient to photocopy and fill in some of the schedule charts in longhand, since the information will change from day to day or week to week.

These forms will be presented in the order in which they were found in the book. Below is a listing of each form, preceded by the page it is on, and followed by the page in which it is described in the book.

- Page 132: *Agency Spec Letter* — refer to pages 23 - 31 in the book.

- Page 133: *Au Pair Arrival Announcement* — refer to page 45 in the book.

- Page 134: *Post Arrival Checklist* — refer to page 49 in the book.

- Page 135: *Week at a Glance Chart* — refer to page 89 in the book.

- Page 136: *Daily Schedule Chart* — refer to page 91 in the book.

- Page 137: *Four Weeks at a Glance Chart* (with "Categories") — refer to page 92.

- Page 138: *Four Weeks at a Glance Chart* (without "Categories") — refer to page 92.

- Page 139: *Month at a Glance Chart* — refer to page 93 in the book.

- Page 140: *Year at a Glance Chart* — refer to page 94 in the book.

- Page 141: *Repeated Event Form* — refer to page 95 in the book.

- Page 142: *Emergency Phone Contact List* — refer to page 96 in the book.

- Page 143: *Checklist for the First Few Weeks* — refer to pages 109 - 110 in the book.

ATTN:
OF:

Subject: Qualities Desired in Our Au Pair

Dear

Following is a description of the qualities that we think will be important to us in choosing an au pair.

- Sex:

- Country of Origin:

- Age Range:

- Family Background:

- Personal Presentation:

- General Activity Level:

- Athletic Abilities:

- Additional Personal Qualities

- Driving Experience:

- Religious Preferences:

- Smoker/Non-Smoker

- Other Issues:

We look forward to seeing the matches that you suggest.

Sincerely,

Date:_____

Dear

On _____, our new au pair is going to arrive. Her name is _____, she is _____ years old, and she hails from _____.

We are excited about this new cross-cultural adventure, and we hope that you'll help us help her to feel at home, when you next see our children.

Best regards,

Post-Arrival Checklist

_____Introduce au pair to neighbors and child's/children's friends and their parents

_____Introduce au pair to child's/children's teachers

_____Get au pair to YMCA, tennis

_____Show au pair how to use all appliances, phones, computer

_____Show au pair how to use the phone, and where the emergency phone list is

_____Introduce au pair to other au pairs

_____Begin driving lessons, and get au pair oriented to the neighborhood

_____Introduce the SOP to the au pair, and give her a copy

_____Set up the weekly schedule, and review it at the end of each week

_____Discuss how we both feel things are going — things that are going well, and things that need to improve

_____House account notebook/recordkeeping

_____ Other:

_____ Other:

_____ Other:

Week of _____ at a Glance

	Before School	School	After School	Evening
Mon.				
Tues.				
Wed.				
Thurs.				
Fri.				
Sat.				
Sun.				

Daily Schedule   Date: _____

7:00 am

8:00 am

9:00 am

10:00 am

11:00 am

12:00 noon

1:00 pm

2:00 pm

3:00 pm

4:00 pm

5:00 pm

6:00 pm

7:00 pm

8:00 pm

9:00 pm

Four Weeks at a Glance   Date:

	Mon	Tues	Wed	Thurs	Fri	Sat	Sun
School							
Shopping							
Afterschool							
Evening							
Other							

	Mon	Tues	Wed	Thurs	Fri	Sat	Sun
School							
Shopping							
Afterschool							
Evening							
Other							

	Mon	Tues	Wed	Thurs	Fri	Sat	Sun
School							
Shopping							
Afterschool							
Evening							
Other							

	Mon	Tues	Wed	Thurs	Fri	Sat	Sun
School							
Shopping							
Afterschool							
Evening							
Other							

Four Weeks at a Glance   Date:

	Mon	Tues	Wed	Thurs	Fri	Sat	Sun

	Mon	Tues	Wed	Thurs	Fri	Sat	Sun

	Mon	Tues	Wed	Thurs	Fri	Sat	Sun

	Mon	Tues	Wed	Thurs	Fri	Sat	Sun

Month at a Glance   Date:

1. _____
2. _____
3. _____
4. _____
5. _____
6. _____
7. _____
8. _____
9. _____
10. _____
11. _____
12. _____
13. _____
14. _____
15. _____
16. _____
17. _____
18. _____
19. _____
20. _____
21. _____
22. _____
23. _____
24. _____
25. _____
26. _____
27. _____
28. _____
29. _____
30. _____
31. _____

About the "Year-at-a-Glance" Form

June

_____

July

_____

August

_____

September

_____

October

_____

November

_____

December

_____

January

_____

February

_____

March

_____

April

_____

May

Event: _____

Contact Information

      Person: _____   Phone: _____

When?

_____

Where?

      Address: _____

Directions:

How Long?

_____

What to Bring:

    • _____   • _____

    • _____   • _____

Other Instructions: _____

_____

EMERGENCY PHONE NUMBERS

In an emergency like a fire or a bad accident at home, call 911 first!

EMERGENCY — 911

After emergency help has been called, call us.   Call 911 first.

Number for M_____

Number for M_____

Car Phone Number _____

What to say if we are at work:

"My name is _____.

I am the _____'s au pair.

This is an emergency.

I must talk to Mr. or Mrs._____ right now."